DATE DUE			
Dec 30			
OCT - 5 1988			
JUN 14 1994			
JUN 24 1994			
			d

BACH, BEETHOVEN, AND BUREAUCRACY:

The Case of the Philadelphia Orchestra

BACH, BEETHOVEN, AND BUREAUCRACY:
The Case of the Philadelphia Orchestra

by

EDWARD ARIAN

THE UNIVERSITY OF ALABAMA PRESS
University, Alabama

To Yvette

Contents

Tables

Preface

A merica today is experiencing a widespread questioning of authority and values. Educational, political, professional, religious, and other institutions are being increasingly subjected to critical examination to determine their responsiveness and relevance in a rapidly changing world. Studies by social scientists are shedding new light upon the dysfunctional aspects of bureaucracy in an attempt to determine just how high a price we have paid for our highly advanced technological and industrial society.

To date, there has been little or no focus upon bureaucratization in our cultural institutions. This study is intended as a contribution in that area. The Philadelphia Orchestra has been selected as the subject of a case study for two reasons: first, it is probably the best known and most successful symphony orchestra in the world; and second, I was for 20 years a member of that orchestra. As such, I was privy to experiences and conversations with Orchestra members, Board members, staff, legal counsel, and union officials of greater depth and frankness than would have been available to any outside investigators. However, I have not relied upon personal experience alone. All the findings have been documented, and the reporting of attitudes and values within the organization is confirmed by the presentation of supplementary material from a professionally-conducted survey and various publications.

It must be stressed that the problems revealed by this study are not peculiar to the Philadelphia Orchestra, but are widespread throughout the American cultural scene. In many instances the Boston Symphony Orchestra, the New York Philharmonic, the Metropolitan Opera Company, or other leading performing arts organizations could serve just as well for illustration. Individuals concerned about the arts in their respective cities across the country, in drama and theater as well as symphony and opera, will recognize, within these pages, a commonalty of problems. The reasons for this are that the social forces controlling the Philadelphia Orchestra have their counterparts in every large community, and the economic forces are national in character.

The decade of the sixties witnessed the achievement of public subsidy for the arts. The decade of the seventies will see a twofold struggle: the first, to increase substantially government appropriations in this area; the second, and equally important, to determine who gets the money and how it is used. This book, therefore, was not approached in the spirit of an expose, but with a concern for both the future of such organizations and the effective use of public subsidy. Institutions such as the Philadelphia Orchestra have only begun to realize their potential for artistic and social service, and it is hoped that this study will help them to do so.

I wish to make a special acknowledgment to my friend and teacher, Professor Peter Bachrach. He was one of those who aided and encouraged me in the occupational switch from musician to political scientist; and he always found time within a busy and hectic schedule to discuss with me at length the ideas and insights out of which this work grew. In so doing, he provided that combination of encouragement and criticism which can only come from a warm personality and a sharp and incisive mind.

Plymouth Meeting, Pa.   EDWARD ARIAN
June, 1971

BACH, BEETHOVEN, AND BUREAUCRACY:

The Case of the Philadelphia Orchestra

Chapter I

Inception And Early History

INCEPTION

The present Philadelphia Orchestra was founded in 1900 under considerable difficulty, and the prospects for its survival were not encouraging. Opera was enjoying much greater public support than symphonic music at that time.[1] The sumptuous Academy of Music at Broad and Locust Streets had been constructed in 1855 principally to house operatic productions. Modeled after the famous La Scala Opera House of Milan, Italy, and boasting a seating capacity of 3,000, it attested to the growing ascendancy of opera in Philadelphia and the United States.[2]

Previous symphonic ensembles in Philadelphia such as the Musical Fund Society Orchestra and the Germania Orchestra had only existed on a limited and tentative basis without having elicited any significant sponsorship or economic support from the community.[3]

In 1881 the eminent musician Theodore Thomas was persuaded to conduct a series of concerts in Philadelphia on a profit-sharing basis with a view to establishing a permanent orchestra of major professional caliber. Public response was poor, however, and after four seasons and a total profit of twenty-eight dollars, the project was abandoned.[4]

In addition to public apathy, moreover, there were other ominous portents for the new Philadelphia Orchestra. Overt opposition to the establishment of a major symphony orchestra existed,[5] and even among its proponents there was bitter dissension and factionalism over the selection of a Musical Director.[6]

The orchestra could only be launched under the guise of a patriotic benefit, and Francis Wister's description of the occasion conveys the existing climate:

> Philadelphians generally do not know that the Philadelphia Orchestra first appeared in this City of Brotherly Love in disguise, a patriotic one, but none-the-less, a disguise. Had it tried to stalk boldly through the city gates, it would have been riddled by the guns of a critical public which disagreed at every point when a permanent orchestra was discussed.
>
> The fact was not made public that these concerts for the benefit of the families of American soldiers and sailors fallen in the Philippines were a preliminary experiment, but on November 16, 1900, as a result of their success, the first concert of the Philadelphia Orchestra took place.[7]

From 1900 to 1912, under the conductorships of Fritz Scheel (1900–1907) and Karl Pohlig (1907–1912), the Philadelphia Orchestra struggled for existence. Although the musical quality of the Orchestra was approved by the local critics,[8] neither Scheel nor Pohlig were glamorous figures with public appeal, and their programming was not considered to be imaginative.[9] As a result, Philadelphians did not respond in terms of financial support or concert attendance. The history of these early years is one of increasing deficits, recurrent financial crises, and poor attendance. It was not uncommon for the Orchestra to draw audiences of 600 people in a hall seating 3,000.[10] The organization was not only unsuccessful at the box office; it failed to generate any significant economic support among the financial aristocracy of Philadelphia.

During these years, and until 1916, a small group of donors and members of the Women's Committees supplied the money to keep the spark alive. They could not know that within a few years the conjunction of Leopold Stokowski and the Philadelphia Orchestra would kindle that spark into a flame which would fire the public imagination, light up the musical world, and, most importantly in organizational terms, open the coffers of moneyed Philadelphia.

THE STOKOWSKI ERA

Leopold Stokowski, the new young conductor from Cincinnati, descended upon Philadelphia on October 12, 1912 with a series of startling announcements concerning his future plans for the Orchestra which "almost took away the breath of the Board of Directors."[11] These plans contained, according to the complaint of one distressed newspaper, "an embarrassing number of novelties."[12] This evidently succeeded, however, in immediately capturing public interest because his first concert at the Academy of Music was completely sold out, and extra chairs had to be placed in the pit adjoining the stage to accommodate the overflow.[13] Moreover, from that point on, large audiences, fascinated by Stokowski's personality as well as curious about his concerts, continued to flock to the Academy of Music.[14]

Stokowski thus demonstrated from the moment of his arrival in Philadelphia and continuously thereafter that he possessed two traits essential to the charismatic leader who serves as a catalyst for great change: the ability to command a following by the force of his personality, and the imagina-

tion which soars above tradition and routine.[15] Experimentation and innovation, combined with a dynamic personality, resulted in a revolution in the status and fortunes of
the Philadelphia Orchestra and the musical life of the city.

The single event which at one stroke brought the Philadelphia Orchestra and its young conductor to international
attention and marked a turning point in the fortunes of that
organization was the American premiere in the spring of
1916 of Gustav Mahler's monumental *Eighth Symphony*,
the "Symphony of 1000," a work requiring in actuality 1,000
performers.

Stokowski had proposed the venture a year before, re-
questing an initial outlay of $15,000 and a year of inter-
mittent rehearsal for preparation. After some hesitation, and
with a certain amount of trepidation, the Board of Directors
gave approval for the project. The Philadelphia Orchestra
Chorus was established, and required almost three months
of auditioning and selection to fill out its roster of 800 voices.
A special platform for this huge chorus took six weeks to
construct and cost $3,000, not including the additional cost
of a wooden apron which had to be added to the stage to
accommodate the enlarged orchestra. Rehearsals began in
October and continued until the performances in March.

Success was instantaneous. There were nine performances
in Philadelphia to a total of 25,000 listeners with an overflow
of 10,000 unfilled orders. Celebrities attended from all over
the country. The orchestra manager jubilantly declared there
was "as much enthusiasm over this work—as one might
expect over a championship baseball series."[16]

After wide publicity and critical acclaim, the entire production was shipped to New York on two private trains
totaling seventeen cars. Speculators there were charging
$25.00 for a ticket as the excitement and anticipation
mounted. The performance, before an audience containing

the musical elite of America, was an even greater success than it had been in Philadelphia.[17]

One symphonic historian declared, "The event catapulted the city, the orchestra, and the young conductor into an intoxicating position of notoriety from which each and all distilled the last ounce of profit."[18] The Philadelphia Chamber of Commerce resolved that the Orchestra was "a commercial asset to the city, rendering it thereby more attractive to visitors, a better home for its citizens, and of greater value to the nation."[19] At one stroke, Stokowski had made the Orchestra an integral part of the city because "never before had there been such a genius for publicity who extended the functional boundaries of a concert so far into nonmusical realms. It was a civic enterprise in which 1,000 citizens cooperated in the actual performance, in which commercial and cultural interests were well mobilized, and in which, still more miraculously, each interest was completely satisfied with the results."[20]

This marked a turning point in the Orchestra's financial fortunes. Two endowment drives were launched which achieved considerable success. Meuller points out: "The Orchestra was lifted from its sixteen-year-old status of a stepchild, during which the story [was] one of constant begging on the part of everybody connected with the institution, to a position of strength from which it was able to launch two endowment campaigns netting nearly two million dollars within seven years."[21]

Stokowski's power of artistic decision-making now became more firmly established by virtue of the fact that he succeeded in attracting a new and powerful type of organizational support, the tycoon-philanthropist. These individuals, mostly first generation descendants of great fortunes founded after the Civil War or the creators themselves of new wealth, were at this time moving into social recognition in Philadelphia. Patronage of the arts was one means of achieving this.[22] Attracted by Stokowski's personality and impressed by the new-found prestige of the Philadelphia Orchestra for which he was responsible, men of great personal wealth now opened their pocketbooks on the condition that he remain at the helm of the Orchestra, and that he be given a free hand.[23]

Stokowski utilized this power during his tenure of almost a quarter of a century and achieved an impressive record of experimentation and innovation, thus enhancing the reputation of the Orchestra.

At the close of the 1914–15 season, at Stokowski's insistence, two weeks of "pops" concerts were added. Patrons at the staid Academy of Music were startled to see that a temporary flooring had been constructed on the parquet circle over which waiters scurried among 200 tables as they served refreshments.[24] This was followed by another innovation for Philadelphia—a series of Children's Concerts which Stokowski inaugurated by bringing a live elephant on stage.[25]

His imagination, however, ranged in even more far-reaching directions than the above. Long before any others, Stokowski grasped the possibilities for applying modern technology to the symphony orchestra. In 1930, the Philadelphia Orchestra performed the first commercially sponsored symphonic broadcasts which were carried coast to coast by 50 radio stations and relayed by short wave to Europe, South America, and Asia.[26] In 1932, the Orchestra pioneered experimentation with symphonic phonograph records at the fledgling RCA studios in Camden, New Jersey, and was the first such organization to be featured on a commercial recording. Anticipating by more than forty years the current interest in combining symphonic music with audio-visual equipment in a mixed media approach, the indefatigable maestro experimented with lighting effects and electrical instruments during concerts,[27] all of which created considerable public interest. Later, the production of *Fantasia* (an animated color film illustrating a concert) was a great popular success which brought symphonic music and the names of Leopold Stokowski and the Philadelphia Orchestra to untold millions of people who had never set foot in a concert hall.

At one point, even the symphony orchestra itself became an inadequate instrument for the free play of Stokowski's restless musical imagination. In 1924, in addition to his orchestral duties, he formed and led, with great public fanfare, the Philadelphia Gold Band of 120 musicians, resplendent in brilliant uniforms. Orchestral music which had been rescored for band was performed to illustrate new tonal possibilities.[28]

During all of this time the colorful maestro never relinquished his charismatic hold upon his audience. These ranged from the proper dowagers whose limousines lined Locust Street on Friday afternoons to the shivering students who waited for hours before a concert on wintry Saturday nights in hopes of purchasing inexpensive seats in the "peanut gallery" at the farthest reaches of the Academy. The Orchestra concerts were sold out in Philadelphia and elsewhere. In New York, by 1923, there was a waiting list of 800 for concert subscriptions.[29]

Part of this appeal was his disdain for many of the traditional aspects of symphonic procedure and protocol. Each new unorthodoxy provoked a "dither of delight" from his devoted followers.[30] At times it took the form of a lecture from the podium, scolding his audience for its reluctance to listen to contemporary works. Occasionally, if the expressions of disapproval of a new work grew too vociferous, Stokowski would retaliate by immediately performing it again.[31] He abandoned the traditional baton and further dazzled music

lovers by committing whole programs to memory, an un-
heard of feat in those days. Once concert goers were
astounded to hear Stokowski denounce applause as a "relic
of the dark ages" and propose an audience referendum on
its abolition.[32]

The Orchestra itself was a constant focus of attention in
Stokowski's relentless search for improvement. There was a
continuous reshuffling of the instrumental choirs in experi-
mental attempts to improve the balance and tonal quality.
Free bowing was introduced among the string players to
encourage independence and originality and increase the
volume of tone. Incentive was maintained among the violinists by giving each player a turn in the concertmaster
position.

The area of programming, however, more than any other
facet of organizational operation, presented Stokowski with
constant opportunities for experimentation and innovation
which he did not hesitate to utilize. He introduced to
American audiences for the first time such now-recognized
masterpieces as Sibelius' *Fifth Symphony*, Schoenberg's *Five
Pieces for Orchestra*, Stravinsky's *Sacre du Printemps*, De
Falla's *El Amor Brujo*, and Mussorgsky's *Boris Godunov*. The
Shostakovitch violin concerto received its world premiere in
Philadelphia. Moreover, Stokowski did not hesitate to undertake the presentation of monumental works, not usually
heard because of the large forces which they required, such
as Stravinsky's *Oedipus Rex*, Prokofieff's *Pas d'Acier*, and
Schoenberg's *Gurrelieder*. Not content with the traditional
symphonic format, the maestro's restless imagination hit
upon the idea of combination orchestra-opera concerts,
which featured among other notable performances Wagner's
Tristan und Isolde. This format was also utilized to give the
American premieres of Schoenberg's *Der glückliche Hand*,

Berg's *Wozzeck,* Stravinsky's *Mavra,* and Gluck's *Iphigenie in Aulis.*[33]

At this point some more systematic evaluation of Stokowski's programming would be helpful for characterizing his era. The programming of a symphonic organization can serve as an important tool for understanding its operational philosophy because programming can serve different goals. It can be designed primarily to entertain and sell tickets; it can attempt to educate and stimulate audiences; it may aspire to high esthetic standards by seeking balance and freshness in the compositions presented; or it may, by granting generous representation to the new and the unfamiliar, conceive of its role as that of the champion of the creative and innovative forces of music. Moreover, since this study proposes to trace a bureaucratization of the Philadelphia Orchestra subsequent to the Stokowski era, any systematic method of program evaluation utilized at this point can also be applied to a later period to help determine whether its programming reflects changes in operational philosophy and what these might be.

The qualitative analysis of symphonic programs, however, presents a problem in that the value judgments of the evaluator cannot be eliminated. Someone must decide, for example, what the categories for evaluation shall be. In any attempt to submit these categories to quantitative calculation, the researcher is still faced with the necessity for making personal judgments. If we wish, for example, to measure service to contemporary music, who deserves classification as a truly contemporary composer, and who does not? The chronological age of a work cannot in itself be any indication of how well it represents contemporary trends inasmuch as there are no objective definitive guidelines as to what constitutes the new or the old in music. As another example, in attempting to characterize programs, what constitutes an imaginative program, an esthetically pleasing program, or an educational program? From another aspect, how many times does a composition have to have been previously performed before it is considered hackneyed or trite?

It was finally decided that if value judgments could not be eliminated they must at least come from highly qualified sources, and that even then they could not be accorded validity unless they demonstrated a high degree of correlation. Four publicly recognized musical experts whose professional specializations included composition, music education, and musical criticism were selected to comprise an evaluating panel. None of them had ever at any time maintained any official connections with the Philadelphia Orchestra. In order to encourage full freedom of expression, anonymity was guaranteed.

Six sample seasons, three from the Stokowski era and three from the post-Stokowski era, were submitted to the panel. In each era the sample seasons were separated by an approximate ten-year period. The panel agreed to evaluate the following categories: (1) originality and imagination, (2) representation of contemporary works, (3) balance of the familiar and the unfamiliar, (4) educational value for audiences, (5) avoidance of hackneyed or trite works of the period. The categories were graded as Excellent, Good, Fair, or Poor.

TABLE I-1

OVERALL EVALUATION FOR THE STOKOWSKI ERA:
SEASONS 1915–1916; 1925–1926; 1934–1935

	Expert-A	Expert-B	Expert-C	Expert-D
1. Originality and imagination	Excellent	Excellent	Good	Excellent
2. Representation of contemporary works	Good	Good	Good	Good
3. Balance of the familiar and the unfamiliar	Excellent	Good	Good	Excellent
4. Educational value for audiences	Excellent	Excellent	Excellent	Excellent
5. Avoidance of hackneyed or trite works of the period	Good	Good	Good	Good

The results for the Stokowski era can be seen in Table I-1. There was unanimity in judging the educational value of the sample programs to be Excellent. Three of the four evaluators felt that their originality and imagination were also Excellent. All agreed that the representation of contemporary works and the avoidance of hackneyed or trite works was Good. Opinion was evenly divided between Excellent and Good on the area of balance of the familiar and the unfamiliar. Over-all, there were nine Excellent and ten Good ratings with no evaluator having judged that any category was less than Good.

Thus, in its programming as well as its other aspects, the operational philosophy of the Stokowski era was characterized by a high degree of freedom of artistic originality and imagination, a dedication to educate audiences about new and broader aspects of music, and an avoidance of the commonplace and the routine.

This, then, was a genuinely charismatic situation. Stokowski not only possessed that "gift of grace"[34] which caused people to follow and support him, but his tenure personified those dichotomies which, according to Max Weber, are always called forth by charismatic leadership: ". . . the 'routine' versus the 'creative' entrepreneur, the conventions of ordinary people versus the inner freedom of the pioneering and exceptional man, institutional rules versus the spontaneous individual, the drudgery and boredom of ordinary existence versus the imaginative flight of the genius."[35] The final requirement of genuinely charismatic leadership, in Weber's theory, is that it must constitute a revolutionary force.[36] In this sense, Stokowski took an infant organization struggling for existence at a time when it represented a neglected art form and catapulted it to cultural predominance and the pinnacle of world prestige and recognition. This was his revolution and his legacy.

THE DEPARTURE OF STOKOWSKI

Ultimately the departure of Stokowski was brought on by changing economic conditions such as the progressive income tax and the Great Depression of 1929. These caused a decline in large individual philanthropy and thereby weakened his base of power. By the end of 1930 one of his principal financial supporters, Edward Bok, was gone, and by the end of 1933 the other, Alexander Van Renssellaer, had followed. In addition to a decline in contributions, the depression had also caused, by 1932, a drop in season subscriptions of fifteen percent.

During this period the members of the Orchestra had accepted a ten percent reduction in salary to help the Association through its financial crisis. At the same time Stokowski was deriving an income estimated at somewhere between $200,000 and $250,000 per year from his position of leadership—about three times that of the President of the United States. His fee to the Association was $2,000 per concert plus an expense account and the maintenance of a private staff.[37]

By 1935, with the disappearance of the large individual contributors from the Board who had constituted Stokowski's principal followers, power passed to a new group of Board members.[38] Their principal concern was whether, under the new economic realities of life, the institution could continue to afford Stokowski and survive. Moreover, friction developed between the new Directors and the fiery conductor over the feasibility of expensive new ventures such as tours of South America and Europe, upon which he was insisting.[39]

Finally, in a move calculated to frighten the Board and bring them to heel, Stokowski tendered his resignation. To his surprise, it was accepted.[40] Thus an era ended.

The deposing of Stokowski can be traced to the inherent instability of charismatic authority. Weber declared:

> By its very nature, the existence of charismatic authority is specifically unstable. . . . The charismatic leader gains and maintains authority solely by proving his strength in life . . . he must perform miracles . . . he must perform heroic deeds. Above all, however, his divine mission must 'prove' itself in that those who faithfully surrender to him must fare well. If they do not fare well, he is obviously not the master sent by the gods . . . the chieftain is often enough simply deserted if success does not remain faithful to him.[41]

When, under the conditions brought about by severe economic depression, the existence of the Philadelphia Orchestra was threatened, it became obvious that Stokowski had run out of miracles. Moreover, it was not to be expected that he would bend to circumstances because charismatic authority abhors ordered economy.[42] Therefore, his insistence that the Orchestra continue to undertake expensive and daring ventures such as the tours to South America and Europe was completely in character. Yet, in the 1930's it flew in the face of harsh economic realities. When this happened, the material interests of the institution which he had created became paramount and he had to go.

This phenomenon, wherein a genuinely charismatic situation gives way before institutional needs as determined by surrounding circumstances, particularly those of the economic order, has been characterized by Weber as the routinization of charisma.[43] He observed "The routinization of charisma, in quite essential respects, is identical with adjustment to the conditions of the economy, that is, to the continuously effective routines of workaday life. In this, the economy leads and is not led."[44]

This process wherein organizational policies and procedures are rationalized and routinized to conform to economic necessity is what is meant by bureaucratization.[45] Economy and efficiency, the deadly enemies of unstructured charismatic leadership, become the ascendant values.

Chapter II

Bureaucratization[1]

THE SELECTION OF STOKOWSKI'S SUCCESSOR

E conomics was undoubtedly a major consideration in the selection of Stokowski's successor. For one thing, the salary of Eugene Ormandy, in contrast to that of his predecessor, greatly reduced the burden upon the Association's budget.[2] The year following his employment, the Association, after eight consecutive years of deficits and with no discernible increase in revenue, showed its first surplus.[3]

The selection of a Musical Director of equal stature to Stokowski would have entailed another large salary, whereas Eugene Ormandy was then only a young conductor with a minor orchestra. The Board was not only seeking someone who could maintain the artistic standards of the organization, but it was also interested in securing the necessary cooperation from a new conductor in effectuating new economic policies: in programming with more box office appeal; in reducing extra rehearsals and overtime by limiting the presentation of new and unfamiliar works; in the restriction of costly artistic productions; and in increasing revenue by utilizing more of the weekly services as concerts rather than rehearsals. The Board was also interested in producing more records faster and, therefore, at less cost, and in more advantageous recording and broadcasting fee arrangements for the Association than had been possible with Stokowski.

In all these matters the Board received infinitely greater cooperation from Ormandy than they had ever received from his volatile predecessor. Board members not only point out that he has maintained the artistic quality and reputation of the Orchestra, but also speak glowingly of his complete dedication to the institution and his willingness to adjust to its economic needs.[4] Here, then, in contrast to the popular caricature of the prima donna conductor, is a critical ingredient of successful bureaucratization, the "organization man" as set forth by Whyte and Presthus, the individual who internalizes the values and goals of the leadership with unswerving loyalty and sets them above all other considerations.[5] He is the embodiment of the successful administrator whose outlook is primarily economic, utilitarian, and pragmatic rather than esthetic or idealistic. Presthus points out:

> Such upward-mobile types personify organizational values. The true 'bureaucratic personality,' they accept the organization's latent goals of power, growth, and survival. . . . Although other members may reject its collective values, the upward-mobiles are deeply committed to them. If they are to succeed, they must accept such values uncritically. They are intensely subject to organizational discipline.[6]

To such persons the bureaucratic milieu is a compatible one; therefore, it is not by accident that the Ormandy era has been marked by a smooth working relationship with the Board, and that his tenure of over 30 years is the longest of any conductor with a major orchestra in the United States.

PROGRAMMING FOR THE BOX OFFICE

Stokowski had been adamant "to the point of intense disagreement with the management" about an organizational responsibility for the performance of contemporary and unfamiliar music.[7] His successor, on the other hand, saw program building primarily as a public relations task governed by the dictates of the box office. He declared:

> No matter what you play, someone doesn't like it. Almost every mail brings a few [sic] complaints to my desk, and more come to the manager's office. But no two complaints are ever alike. So what am I to do? What patron shall I please?[8]

The Association sees Ormandy's programming as "a judicious middle-of-the-road course," and candidly explains:

> Whatever a conductor's desire to promote new works and give new talent a hearing, he is invariably governed to some degree by the strictly commercial aspect of his selection, meaning the box office appeal (or lack of it).[9]

His approach is summed up by the association as "no stunts, no loud noises, nothing to offend."[10]

Ormandy's first concert program was a great success with concertgoers because, as one reporter put it, in obvious comparison with his predecessor, "The audience was genuinely pleased to hear a program of beautiful music instead of foundry imitations and noises from the nethermost depths." The new conductor, he went on, "seemed to find a responsive chord in his listeners. They no longer leave because they don't like what they hear."[11] Moreover, Ormandy's programming policies have continued to be successful at the box office for over 30 years, and have represented an important financial contribution to the organization.

This success, however, has not been attained without cost.

For example, it is a widely accepted fact that many works of art which have been truly creative or innovative have generated controversy and given offense. The history of creative expression of all forms abounds with too many examples to bear repetition here. Beethoven, Brahms, and Wagner, to mention only a few in music, were, at one time or another, controversial composers. If a symphonic organization adopts a policy of playing nothing to offend its audiences out of commercial considerations, it need hardly be added that it runs the risk of automatically excluding many vital contemporary works. In addition, from an educational standpoint, it would appear that this policy will hardly advance the level of audience appreciation or stir it from a somnolent lethargy. As recently as 1968, a leading Philadelphia music critic wrote of the 1967–68 concert season:

> Programs heard during the season again place the Philadelphians among the most conservative and least adventurous of major orchestras. But it seems the public would have it so and the managment is only too happy to acquiesce.[12]

The Use of Programming to Maximize Record Royalties

In 1943, the Philadelphia Orchestra Association discontinued its relationship with the RCA Victor Company which had been in effect during the Stokowski era. A new contract to record exclusively for Columbia Records was consummated.[13] The agreement, which lasted for 24 years with renewals, called for the Association and the Musical Director to receive a specified royalty on each record sold. The result was a prodigious outpouring of records. During the period 1940 to 1949, 24 million Philadelphia Orchestra records were sold. By 1950, the Orchestra had the largest recorded repertory of any existing orchestra, and its sales throughout the world were unsurpassed.[14] *Billboard,* the magazine known as the "bible of the recording industry," reported in 1962 that Eugene Ormandy (who only recorded with the Philadelphia Orchestra) was the top selling classical artist at Columbia Records, and that he and the Philadelphia Orchestra had "topped" all other "classical acts" according to a seven-month poll of record dealers across the United States.[15]

The income derived from record royalties has become an economic cornerstone of the organization. Two recent financial statements of the Association show this sum to be in excess of a quarter of a million dollars, or more than fourteen percent of the Orchestra's earned income.[16] Moreover, this figure may be too low. Details of the recording agreement are not available, but knowledgeable observers point out that if certain bookkeeping and deferred payment arrangements are being used, the actual annual royalty income could be higher. In addition, Columbia has a backlog of unreleased records which represents additional royalties as it is fed into the market. In any event, the dependence upon record royalties is considerable. In 1962, the manager of the Orchestra told a congressional subcommittee, "If those royalties go down, we are in trouble."[17]

The Association, therefore, has adopted operational policies designed to insure that these royalties do not go down. Two requirements for survival in modern organizational society are the control to the greatest possible extent of both the cost of and the demand for one's product. This involves, in the first instance, maximum economy and efficiency in production, and, in the second instance, the use of means which create and continue to stimulate demand.[18] This essentially is how the Philadelphia Orchestra Association has utilized its concert programming.

In the first instance, the procedure for reducing the cost

of record production is to program a work scheduled for recording on concerts which immediately precede or are as close as possible to the date of the recording session. In this way it becomes possible to thoroughly rehearse the work, ostensibly for the concerts but in actuality for the recording, at no additional cost above the musicians' normal weekly wage, which includes concerts but not recording sessions. Once at the recording session, the taping of the work consumes a minimum of time inasmuch as it is well prepared. This reduces the labor cost of the recording because the musicians are paid on an hourly basis. The end result is a boost in record royalties because these labor costs are recoverable by the recording company from the gross sale of records before the royalties of the Association or the conductor are calculated.

In the second instance, record sales are stimulated by performing works from the record catalog while at the same time indicating in the program booklet or elsewhere that the recorded performance by the Orchestra is available.

To mathematically assess the extent to which programming serves both to reduce the costs of record production and to stimulate the sale of records, two sample seasons, 1960–61 and 1961–62, were selected for analysis.

The 1960–61 season contained a total of 199 compositions. Of these, 31 were to be recorded, and 71 served as advertisements for the recording catalog. Thus, fifty-one percent of the programming that season served to maximize record royalties.

In the 1961–62 season, 222 compositions were programmed, of which 24 were to be recorded and 57 were advertisements of the recording catalog. Thus, thirty-seven percent of programming that season served to maximize record royalties.

In summation, the analysis of the above sample seasons

demonstrates that an average of almost one out of every two compositions programmed (forty-four percent) served as an economic aid to recording.

There remains, however, the question of the cost involved. Inasmuch as the recording company is a profit-making organization and the royalties of the Association and the conductor are based upon unit sales, it must be assumed that, at the very least, there exists a strong motivation on the part of all parties concerned for the maximum sale of records. Since the public buys what it is most familiar with and likes best, there is a strong inclination to cater to mass demand by programming and recording those compositions with the greatest popular appeal. Conservative audience tastes are at once created, sustained, and catered to, and a circle of conservatism is completed and continues to feed upon itself.

The Use of Programming
to Permit a Maximum Number of Concerts

A third area of operation which utilizes programming as an aid is the Orchestra scheduling of rehearsals and concerts. The union contract allows for eight weekly services, of which any number may be rehearsals and up to four may be concerts. Not included within these eight services are Pension Fund concerts, Children's Concerts, or recording sessions. The economic policies of the Association dictate that the maximum number of allowable concerts be utilized at all times in order to maximize revenue, and this policy has been adhered to. Moreover, considerations of economy require that there be little or no expenditure for overtime or extra rehearsals. This leaves four two-and-one-half hour rehearsals per week.

It must not be assumed, however, that even this small

amount of rehearsal time is completely available for the preparation of the weekly program. The following representative weekly Orchestra schedule is self-explanatory:

Monday—10:30 to 1:00 rehearsal

This rehearsal is mostly taken up with the further polishing of the previous week's program, which is to be repeated that evening and again on Tuesday evening before the influential critics in New York. In addition, if it is being recorded on Wednesday, which is often the case, rehearsal is especially necessary.

Tuesday—3:30 to 6:00 rehearsal in New York (previous week's program)

This is necessary to allow balancing and adjustment to the different accoustics of an unfamiliar concert hall, especially if there is a choral work on the program or the accompaniment of a soloist. The final hour of this rehearsal may be devoted to the coming weekend program.

8:30 concert (previous week's program)

Wednesday—recording session

Thursday—10:30 to 1:00 rehearsal

Sometimes an hour of this rehearsal may have to be allotted for the preparation of an upcoming Children's Concert on Saturday morning, which does not feature the program.

Friday—10:00 to 12:30 rehearsal
2:30 concert

Saturday—11:00 Children's Concert
8:30 concert

At all rehearsals a fifteen-minute intermission is required. Thus, a total of four and one-half hours for the week can be devoted to the preparation of the weekend program.

To make this scheduling feasible, the Orchestra repeatedly

programs standard works with which it is familiar, and which, therefore, it can prepare within the allotted time.

The cost, in this instance, is obviously a severe limitation upon the type of work which can be programmed. Since the presentation of a new or unfamiliar major work requires, even in the case of a highly-skilled professional organization, a considerable amount of rehearsal time, the production of this type of work is relatively rare over the course of each season.

Some Orchestra weekly schedules may not follow the above one, but because of the ever-present combinations of travel requirements, recording sessions, Pension Fund concerts, Children's Concerts, and a full concert schedule, the harried aspect of a minimum of rehearsals for concert preparation rarely changes. The result is that freshness, innovation, audience education, and the representativeness of new works in programming are the continuing casualties.

In Chapter I a method of program evaluation involving a panel of musical experts and sample programs of the Stokowski and the post-Stokowski eras was formulated.[19] It will be recalled that the Stokowski era was found to have been imaginative, educational, and innovative in programming,[20] thus furnishing support for the characterization of his era as a genuinely charismatic one. In Table II–1, the results are presented which emerged from the same panel concerning the post-Stokowski (Ormandy) era.

Opinion was evenly divided between Fair and Poor as to originality and imagination. The representation of contemporary works was somewhat above Poor with three votes being Poor and one Fair, while the balance of the familiar and the unfamiliar was slightly below Fair with three votes being Fair and one Poor. Most striking of all, however, was the unanimous evaluation of Poor as to both educational value for audiences and the avoidance of hackneyed or trite works of the period. There were overall 14 grades of Poor and six grades of Fair, with no Good or Excellent gradings in any category.

These results furnish additional evidence that the efficient use of programming in all the ways enumerated above to meet economic imperatives has, at the same time, exacted a heavy toll in program quality and audience education.

TABLE II-1
OVERALL EVALUATION FOR THE POST-STOKOWSKI (ORMANDY) ERA: SEASONS 1941–42; 1951–52; 1961–62

	Expert–A	Expert–B	Expert–C	Expert–D
1. Originality and imagination	Poor	Poor	Fair	Fair
2. Representation of contemporary works	Poor	Poor	Poor	Fair
3. Balance of the familiar and the unfamiliar	Fair	Fair	Poor	Fair
4. Educational value for audiences	Poor	Poor	Poor	Poor
5. Avoidance of hackneyed or trite works of the period	Poor	Poor	Poor	Poor

SOME ADDITIONAL COSTS OF MAXIMIZING RECORD ROYALTIES

The recording royalties which have helped to sustain the Philadelphia Orchestra have entailed other costs in addition to programming. For one thing, they have strongly influenced the selection of concert soloists. Most established soloists are under exclusive contract to one record company. A large share of the recorded orchestral accompaniments of the artists under exclusive contract to Columbia Records has been performed by the Philadelphia Orchestra. This has necessitated the presentation of these artists at concerts prior to the recording sessions in order to save recording costs. As a result, Philadelphia, according to one music critic, has become known as a "Columbia town" where for many years artists under exclusive contract to record companies other than Columbia were simply not available to the audiences of the Philadelphia Orchestra, who have had to settle for a considerably narrowed range of concert artists. In the 1967–68 season the Orchestra switched to an exclusive recording agreement with RCA Victor, and one Board member was moved to candidly comment, "It will be a pleasure to hear some RCA artists for a change." It can also be predicted, however, that the appearances of Columbia artists in Philadelphia will now become increasingly scarce.

The concentration upon producing records as quickly and economically as possible has also had discernible effects upon the morale of the members of the Orchestra. The deeper implications of bureaucratization for labor relations will be dealt with in another chapter. The purpose here is simply to illustrate some of the recording practices which have aroused resentment among the musicians of the Orchestra.

Principally, Orchestra members feel that recording sessions are hurried with one eye on the clock in a way which they feel is demeaning to their artistic sensibilities. They complain of a feeling of being "pushed along" which is incompatible with making great music. They speak of being severely rebuked for an involuntary error which necessitates the expense of retaping a fragment of music, whereas the same error at a concert or rehearsal does not call forth a similar reaction. On the other hand, first chair players, who feel that their professional reputations are dependent upon the solo passages which become permanent on records, express bitterness that they are sometimes given only one chance to record a passage because of the cost involved.

For another thing, the union contract provides that only those who have performed a work in concert need be engaged for the recording of the work. A smaller number of players for the recording of a composition naturally means less cost. Orchestra members declare that the result at times has been a reduction in the number of players at concert performances, particularly in the accompaniments of soloists, not out of musical considerations but in preparation for the recording session. This practice has been the subject of several grievances presented to the union and has led to direct confrontations between the Musical Director and the Orchestra members' committee. Several former committee members claim to have kept records showing that the number of players for a particular composition has varied from season to season, depending upon whether or not it was to be recorded. All in all, there exists a strong cynicism among Orchestra members which holds that artistic ideals and dedication to music are checked at the door when it comes to the lucrative recording situation.

Another sore point in labor relations attributable partially to the recording situation is the amount of travel which the Orchestra does. Musicians complain about being away excessively from home and family, while the Association insists with equal vehemence upon the need for travel to keep the Orchestra before a wide public and sell records. The Association does not hesitate to state publicly, "The Orchestra's tour activities also serve to promote the sale of phonograph records."[21] Board members and administrative staff claim to have seen statistics which purport to show that, when the Philadelphia Orchestra did not put in a personal appearance in certain geographical areas within a five-year period, the sale of records fell off.

The Philadelphia Orchestra, by its own admission, is the most widely traveled orchestra in the world.[22] It has not been possible to determine to what extent its tours have been subsidized by recording companies, but the Association has stated that at least two transcontinental tours, 1946 and 1947, were sponsored by Columbia Records.[23] When the Orchestra has traveled to Western Europe, there has been close contact with Philips, a European affiliate of Columbia

Records, under whose label the Philadelphia Orchestra records are sold in Europe.

During the strike of 1966, the Orchestra members expressed resentment not only about touring, but also at having to play summer festivals away from Philadelphia, such as the one at Saratoga, New York. Again, as in the case of touring, the Association answers that this is a prestigious activity which aids the sale of records.

This extensive traveling has exacted a heavy toll in labor relations. In both their private and public statements, the members of the Orchestra express a deep resentment over this issue. During the most bitter strikes of the Philadelphia Orchestra, a recurrent and prominent theme has been the charge by Orchestra members that they are compelled to travel to a point of physical and emotional exhaustion.[24]

Another factor which is affected by the recording situation is the relationship between the members of the Orchestra and the Musical Director. Inasmuch as the latter receives a personal royalty on the sale of records, his income from this activity is considerably higher than that of the musician, who is only compensated by an hourly wage. Moreover, the shorter the amount of time consumed in the making of a record, the smaller the income of the musician and the greater the income of the Musical Director inasmuch as the cost of labor is recoverable before royalties begin. Given this situation, there is a strong motivation for the musical Director to at the very least acquiesce, and at the worst enthusiastically engage, in some type of speedup.

Furthermore, there are marketing considerations. Ours is a star-oriented society in which the name often sells the product. In this sense, the conductor becomes a marketable product, and his name on a label, if sufficiently known, can help to sell that record. As a result, a good part of the public relations of the organization is dedicated to building up the public image of the conductor. As the record catalog and record sales have grown, Eugene Ormandy has come more and more to represent to the Association a vested interest whose name must be kept before the public. A labor expert who was involved in the 1966 Orchestra strike declared that the Association was "worried sick" about the hiatus in record royalties which might occur between the time Ormandy retires and the public image of his successor can be built up. This factor, plus box office considerations, accounts for the search today by orchestra associations for conductors whose principal asset is glamor rather than solid musicianship.[25]

However, this glamorization process arouses a natural resentment among the musicians who, understandably, feel that a certain amount of credit for musical preeminence is due to their efforts. When publicity reaches the point where the conductor is quoted as declaring, "There is no Philadelphia sound. There is just the conductor's sound,"[26] tempers in the Orchestra flare.

What should be a close and intimate relationship of colleagues in the making of great music between the Musical Director and the Orchestra is subjected to severe strain. It becomes, as Presthus has suggested of the bureaucratic context, an instrumental and manipulative relationship.[27] This, then, is another factor in a total situation which lowers morale and, as will be shown, has serious implications for labor relations.

INCREASED CONCERTS AND TOURING

It has been previously pointed out that a bureaucratic policy of economy and efficiency has dictated that the Association use the greatest possible amount of labor services for concerts rather than apportioning those services between rehearsals and concerts in a manner which would permit more varied programs. This has been another factor, along with the need to stimulate record sales, which has made for increased touring because the local market for concert activity, as visualized by the Association, is small and quickly saturated. That is to say, the Association considers the local market to consist only of those individuals able and willing to pay regular concert prices. Under a policy of maximizing revenue, once this market is exhausted it becomes necessary to expand operations to other cities in order to reach a similar type of customer rather than engage in less remunerative local activities such as educational concerts for youth or low priced concerts for the less advantaged.

The Association itself has characterized the Orchestra as "Traveling Minstrels" and declares, "The Philadelphia Orchestra travels more miles to play more concerts in more different cities to more listeners than any other symphony in the world."[28] From the 1938–39 season (the beginning of the Ormandy era) through the 1948–49 season, the Orchestra traveled 151,000 miles by rail and 6,000 miles by boat. The 1940–41 season was average with 13,565 miles of travel. This average dropped during the war years to 9,130 miles, but by 1948 it was up again to 25,000 miles.[29]

In Table II–2 some sample seasons are analyzed with regard to the total amount of concerts and touring per season. It is significant that the increase in concerts and touring (1938 onward) correlates with the beginning of the Ormandy era and the inception of bureaucratic values of economy and efficiency. Note that in 1934–35 (the end of the Stokowski era) there were 100 concerts in a 33 week season, or an average of about three per week. By 1966–67 the number had risen to 204 concerts in a 48 week season, or an average of four and one-quarter per week. In the 1934–35 season, the union contract allowed nine services per week, of which about thirty-three and one-third percent were concerts. By 1966–67 the union contract had reduced services to eight per week, of which fifty-three percent were now utilized as concerts. Even more striking is the increase in travel. In 1934–35 there were 17 out of 100 concerts played out of town, or a seventeen percent travel factor. By 1966–67 there were 83 concerts of a total of 204 which took place out of town, or a forty percent travel factor. This represents an approximate increase in travel of two hundred thirty percent.

Association spokesmen, in interviews with the author, have disputed the financial advantages of touring, pointing out that the costs of transportation and living expenses on the road are prohibitive. However, since the Philadelphia Orchestra is the most widely-traveled symphony in the world,[30] and at the same time has the highest earned income ratio (eighty-six percent of operating expenses) of any orchestra in the United States,[31] this is open to question. Moreover, it has turned out that touring has brought an additional bonus of increased support from the business community, which views it as a means of advertising Philadelphia.[32] All in all, it would appear that the Association's twin policy of increasing concerts while confining itself to only the most lucrative markets both locally and elsewhere has been an effective economic aid to survival.

The costs, however, have been twofold. First, as previously explained, the travel factor has had an abrasive effect upon labor relations. In the last three strikes which the organization has experienced, the resentment of the Orchestra members over the amount of time spent away from home has been a recurrent theme.[33] Board members as well as union officials acknowledge this to be a major problem of labor relations. Second, because the Orchestra is available to only a relative few in the community who can afford to attend its regularly priced concerts, other large segments of the local population have ben excluded from its cultural benefits.

TABLE II-2
INCREASE IN TOURING

Season	Concerts (Philadelphia)	Concerts (out of town)	Total
1934–35	83	17	100
1935–36	100	16	116
1936–37	72	28	100
1938–39	72	45	117
1939–40	72	69	141
1966–67	121	83	204

ADDITIONAL METHODS OF REDUCING OPERATING COSTS

Some additional areas of operation in which the Association has been able to effect economies have helped to reduce its deficit. Children's Concerts, for example, are an inescapable public obligation, and yet they are even more unprofitable than regular concerts because they require lower admission prices. Until 1967 the Association circumvented this problem by having these concerts performed under auspices of the Philadelphia Orchestra Pension Foundation, wherein the Orchestra members played without compensation and the proceeds went into their pension fund. The Association thus fulfilled a public obligation at no cost to itself. Moreover, the Association, which is actually the owner of the Academy of Music, received full rental fees from the Pension Foundation for these concerts and all other pension concerts. The Orchestra members discontinued this practice in 1967, and the Association must now pay for these concerts. It still minimized its losses here, however, by limiting these concerts to five per year, which is one of the lowest figures in the United States for this type of organization.

The area of retirement benefits is another example of how the Association has met a recognized obligation with a minimum of financial stress. The Philadelphia Orchestra did not start a successful pension plan until 1943, when it was launched upon the initiative of the Orchestra members. The Association contributed one hundred dollars per year per member (changed a few years later to one hundred and fifty and unchanged thereafter until 1960), and the Orchestra members matched this. Approximately eighty percent of the total income of the fund, however, came from activities performed without pay by the Orchestra members, such as pension concerts, Children's Concerts, and recordings. Responsibility for the direction of fund raising was vested in a non-profit foundation with which the Association maintained no formal connections and for which it assumed no financial responsibility. Administrative decision-making for the plan, however, was performed by a joint committee of three Orchestra members, three Board members, and, until 1963, the manager of the Orchestra as an ex officio voting member. In this way, although changes in the conditions of the plan are subject to membership ratification, the Association has been able to exert a dominating influence over the plan while assuming less financial responsibility than the members of the Orchestra themselves.

Since the present pension plan did not start until the Orchestra had been in existence 42 years (a previous plan had failed), there was a considerable amount of past service to be funded. It took almost 18 years to accomplish this, and it too was done principally through the labors of the Orchestra members. In addition, since participation in federal Social Security was at that time voluntary for non-profit employers, the Association met this demand of the Orchestra members by an initial compromise (which continued for several years) wherein its contribution was indirectly paid out of Pension Foundation income.

In addition to the above, there are other examples from a wide spectrum of organizational activities which serve to illustrate the determination of the Association to control its costs and thereby minimize its deficit. The minutes of the Orchestra membership meetings and interviews with union officials, for example, reveal a large catalog of grievances over a sustained period of years, all of which arose out of an unswerving commitment to economy. Included are such items as disputed interpretations of what equipment and conditions constitute first class conditions of travel, disputes over contractual obligations for food allowances while on tour, accusations of dishonesty in timekeeping, and accusations of evasion of payment for a variety of services by distorting contractual provisions.

The cost of all the above economies is obviously found in morale and labor relations. The Orchestra members, for example, bitterly characterize their pension plan as a "do-it-yourself kit." When pension concerts and rehearsals are superimposed upon an already crowded schedule, the situation is further exacerbated. As far as the other grievances listed above, their sheer volume and persistence over a period of years furnish confirmation of a tense labor situation.

The Allocation of Benefits as a Control Mechanism

A phenomenon associated with bureaucracy is the allocation of status, prestige, or financial reward in a manner calculated to control personnel and reduce conflict with the organization over the conditions of their employment.[34] The awarding of privileges or recognition to some employees tends to make them accept the conditions of their work situation and overlook the existence of a general inter-dependence of all employees vis-a-vis the employer. This weakens their united front against him. Moreover, even the militancy of the employee who does not receive these bene-fits may be diluted because he is always tempted by the possibility that if he cooperates with management he may share in them.

The Philadelphia Orchestra Association has applied this policy in three ways. First, there exists in the Orchestra a carefully differentiated allocation of benefits wherein first chair players have been singled out by the management for special treatment in a variety of ways: they receive higher salaries than other Orchestra members; they receive bonuses for the making of records; they are occasionally allowed to perform as soloists at concerts or on records; they are invited to social functions of the Association from which other Orchestra members are excluded; they are mentioned or featured from time to time in Orchestra publicity; they are assigned preferential travel facilities and hotel accommoda-tions; organization rules, in many instances, are waived for them; and, in certain cases, their students are shown prefer-ence in hiring.

The second application of this policy has to do with seat-ing in the string sections. Recognition of individual ability within these large sections is theoretically based upon the distance by chair number from the first chair. Advancement, even from tenth to ninth violin, can be terribly important to the ego of the musician. Moreover, a seat in the first violin section is considered more prestigious than one in the second violins. The Musical Director, in this situation, has complete authority to assign seating and is accountable to no one, which enhances his power considerably.

Third, there are no specified salaries beyond the minimum

for any chair in the Orchestra in the union contract. This means that the Association bestows salaries above the minimum to whom and for whatever reasons it chooses. In this instance also, the Musical Director's recommendation is considered to be the final word.

Recently some inroads upon these prerogatives have been made elsewhere,[35] and the Orchestra members, in recent negotiations for a new labor contract, asked for a voice in a formalized and impersonal promotional procedure. They also asked that a specified salary for each chair in the Orchestra, regardless of occupant, be placed in the union contract. This was vehemently refused, however, by the Association, attesting to the importance which it places upon these control mechanisms.

The resultant cost of this policy has been an exacerbation of the bitterness of those who do not benefit and a worsening of labor relations. Charges of favoritism and politicking against the management, and especially the Musical Director, are rampant. Moreover, in the opinion of some, the policy backfires. It is impossible to substantiate, but some Orchestra members feel that the arbitrary awarding of privileges encourages increased militancy on the theory that the wheel which squeaks the loudest gets the grease. In other words, they feel that the Association may be more inclined to buy off its enemies than to reward its friends, which actually encourages conflict.

ROUTINIZATION

A bureaucracy not only rationalizes operations, it also routinizes them. That is, once efficient and economical methods are developed, they are adhered to on a day-to-day basis.

Table II–3 reveals the extent to which the Philadelphia

Orchestra has succeeded in doing this for almost a quarter of a century. This random sampling of six winter seasons over a twenty-three year period reveals: only three concerts were played in Philadelphia at places other than the Academy of Music; the Friday-Saturday-Monday subscription formula continued without interruption until 1968–69; all concerts in each season have been standard symphonic concerts at regular prices with the exception of three pension concerts, five Children's Concerts, and three Youth Concerts (which were increased to six by 1968–69 when the three pension concerts had been dropped); the large majority of out of town concerts have taken place in the same cities (New York, Washington, and Baltimore) for the same audiences (they are sold on an annual renewable subscription basis).

In the case of routinization, the costs lie not so much in what has been done as in what has not been done. For example, there are no concerts in the sample at schools, hospitals, industrial plants, suburban facilities, or, with four exceptions, at municipal facilities. There is no use of the Orchestra for seminars at educational institutions, or as a forum to enable composers to hear their works. No time has been allotted for the operation of a training orchestra for young aspiring symphony players. There is no utilization of the Orchestra for such socially constructive purposes as ghetto concerts or low priced concerts for less advantaged groups. There has been no attempt to serve the special audience which exists for concerts of a popular nature. Finally, the young audiences have been neglected. The Youth Concerts have never exceeded six per year. Moreover, the number of Children's Concerts has remained at five per year, and since they are sold on a subscription basis for the series, this has meant that they have been available to only about 3,000 children per year in a metropolitan area of over three million population.

TABLE II–3

THE ROUTINIZATION OF OPERATIONS

1945–46 season

28 Friday concerts[a]	3 pension concerts	(Philadelphia)
28 Saturday concerts	5 Children's Concerts	(Academy of Music)
10 Monday concerts	3 Youth Concerts	( )

10 New York (Carnegie Hall)	Worcester one week
8 Washington (Constitution Hall)	Ann Arbor one week
6 Baltimore (Lyric Theatre)	

1947–48 season

28 Friday concerts	3 pension concerts	(Philadelphia)
28 Saturday concerts	5 Children's Concerts	(Academy of Music)
10 Monday concerts	3 Youth Concerts	( )

10 New York (Carnegie Hall)	Worcester one week
8 Washington (Constitution Hall)	Ann Arbor one week
6 Baltimore (Lyric Theatre)	

1950–51 season

28 Friday concerts	3 pension concerts	(Philadelphia)
28 Saturday concerts	5 Children's Concerts	(Academy of Music)
10 Monday concerts	3 Youth Concerts	( )
3 miscellaneous concerts		( )

4 city concerts (Convention Hall)	Worcester one week
10 New York (Carnegie Hall)	Ann Arbor one week
7 Washington (Constitution Hall)	
6 Baltimore (Lyric Theatre)	

1960–61 season

28 Friday concerts	3 pension concerts	(Philadelphia)
28 Saturday concerts	5 Children's Concerts	(Academy of Music)
10 Monday concerts	3 Youth Concerts	( )

10 New York (Carnegie Hall)	Ann Arbor one week
4 Washington (Constitution Hall)	
10 Baltimore (Lyric Theatre)	

1964–65 season

28 Friday concerts	3 pension concerts	(Philadelphia)
28 Saturday concerts	5 Children's Concerts	(Academy of Music)
14 Monday concerts	3 Youth Concerts	( )

10 New York (Lincoln Center)	Ann Arbor one week
8 New York (Carnegie Hall)	tour one week
5 Washington (Constitution Hall)	transcontinental tour six weeks
10 Baltimore (Lyric Theatre)	

TABLE II-3—Cont.

1968–69 season

24 Friday concerts	5 Children's Concerts	(Philadelphia)
24 Saturday concerts	6 Youth Concerts	(Academy of Music)
6 Friday concerts		( )
6 Saturday concerts		( )
14 Monday concerts		( )
14 Thursday concerts		( )
10 New York (Lincoln Center)	Ann Arbor	one week
4 New York (Carnegie Hall)	tour	three weeks
5 Washington (Constitution Hall)		
8 Baltimore (Lyric Theatre)		

ªWith the exception of pension, Children's, Youth, and city concerts, all other concerts in this table have been confirmed as standard symphonic concerts at regular prices.

SOURCE: Philadelphia Orchestra programs

THE FINANCIAL EFFICACY OF THE
ASSOCIATION'S OPERATIONAL POLICIES

The true efficicacy of the Association's operational policies in terms of financial outcomes is difficult to evaluate with complete accuracy inasmuch as its books are not available for public inspection. In fact, its financial condition has been surrounded by secrecy and ambiguity. During the 1966 strike, the Association publicly refused to permit an audit of its books to determine whether it was truly unable to meet the wage demands of the union.[36] Financial statements issued to Association members were described in 1966 as growing "increasingly briefer and more cryptic each year."[37] In the 1964–65 season report, for example, the statement of assets and liabilities was dropped, and in the 1965–66 statement even the accountants' report was omitted.[38] Further, financial statements were consolidated with the Academy of Music of Philadelphia, Inc., thus making it even more difficult to arrive at a clear picture of the condition of the Philadelphia Orchestra Association, Inc. itself.[39] Finally, the practice of having two endowment funds, one restricted (comprised exclusively of funds given to the Association and earmarked by the donor specifically as an endowment contribution), and one unrestricted (wherein any funds given to the Association without stipulation may be transferred to this fund or out again) has given rise to strong suspicion that the unrestricted fund has been used as a convenient device to shift assets around and thereby control loss and surplus statements.

As a result of these policies and the charges of financial manipulation which were made during the 1966 strike, a general attitude of distrust was detected among potential donors. A professional survey commissioned by the Association in preparation for an upcoming capital fund drive (the Philadelphia Orchestra Challenge Program) declared:

> Members of the business community *insist* that they will have to have a much clearer picture of the financial affairs of the Philadelphia Orchestra Association before they can consider any sizable response. The "half knowledge" concerning ownership of the Academy and the land behind it as well as bits of information which came out from time to time during the strike concerning the amount of deficit, the amount of endowment, "why two endowments," and the general charges of secretiveness have left behind a latent suspicion among the members of the business community and a definite feeling that they must have more information and more explanation.[40]

In response to this report and under the imperatives of the Philadelphia Orchestra Challenge Program,[41] the Association subsequently issued more detailed financial statements for the 1966–67 and 1967–68 seasons. Thus, although the books are still not open for public inspection, with the aid of these reports and certain other documented facts it is now possible to arrive at a reasonably accurate evaluation of the efficacy, from a strictly financial standpoint, of the operational policies which have been described in this chapter.

The Association was able to proudly state in 1950 that, although symphony orchestras have deficits, in the case of the Philadelphia Orchestra, "Actually there have been very few years when a public appeal for funds has been made."[42] It pointed out that between the 1938–39 season and the 1948–49 season there had been no public solicitation of funds.[43] The operating deficits had been kept down to a point where they could be raised among "friends" in contrast to going to the general public.[44] Most impressive of all was that in the matter of capital funds the 1967 drive was the first such appeal to the public since 1919.

This impressive record is due to the fact that the Philadelphia Orchestra has had the highest earning ratio of any major symphony in the United States. In 1966 this ratio was eighty-six percent of operating expenses.[45] Moreover, according to the American Symphony Orchestra League, the operating expenses of the Philadelphia Orchestra appear to be the most economical of any major symphony in the United States.[46] In addition, the Association has been able to offset the increased labor costs of its 1966 contract by upping its fees for performances throughout the country, and this has been accepted virtually without question.[47]

At this writing the Philadelphia Orchestra Challenge Program, according to an Association spokesman, is nearing its announced goal of ten million dollars. He explains that the success of the drive has been due largely to the response of the business community, which recognizes that the prestigious activities of the Orchestra constitute an excellent advertisement for the city. He further explains that the drive will now be allowed to end just short of its goal and without publicity. The reason given is that if the drive were allowed to go over the top and so publicized there would be a public assumption of permanent financial security which would tend to discourage future support. Furthermore, the Association fears that such an announcement would have the effect of upgrading the wage demands of the musicians in negotiations for any new labor contract.

Beyond the immediate funds collected in this drive, the Association can expect a continuing benefit. Professional fund raisers for the Association point out that once a corporation makes a policy decision to contribute and budgets for it, it tends to be recurrent.

In Tables II–4 and II–5 are to be found the first complete financial statements of the Association. They cover the 1966–67 and 1967–68 seasons. Several items are noteworthy as indicating a healthy financial condition:

(a) In 1966–67, the Association actually achieved a surplus of $18,412. This was partially due to deferred record royalty payments.

(b) In 1967–68, the deficit was $58,551. If it is assumed that the practice of deferred royalties is continuing, it is possible that there was in actuality little or no deficit again that year.

(c) Over a period of years considerable sums have been expended for the restoration and improvement of the Academy of Music and the purchase of equipment. However no capitalization is shown for this, and it should be noted that exception to this practice is taken in the accountants' report.

(d) Restoration and improvement of the Academy is financed from the proceeds of the Academy Ball Concert, an established annual event of social prominence. It can be assumed that at some point in the near future when this work is completed the proceeds from this event will then be available to the Association for other purposes.

(e) A mortgage, taken from the endowment fund to purchase the Academy of Music, has been reduced to almost half and will be paid up in seven years.

The above serves to illustrate that the Philadelphia Orchestra Association is in good financial condition for a nonprofit organization.

TABLE II–4

THE PHILADELPHIA ORCHESTRA ASSOCIATION
ANNUAL REPORT 1966–67

The Philadelphia Orchestra Association
and
Academy of Music of Philadelphia, Inc.

STATEMENT OF CONSOLIDATED INCOME
Twelve Months Ended August 31, 1967

Orchestra income:			
Concert income	$1,543,967		
Record royalties	269,890		
Television	5,739		
Commercial sponsorship	22,000		
Miscellaneous	5,379	$1,846,975	
Academy income:			
Rentals	$ 265,255		
Other	28,193	293,448	
GROSS INCOME			$2,140,423
Orchestra expenses:			
Musicians, conductors, soloists	$1,458,005		
Transportation and baggage	110,674		
Musicians' travel allowance	183,372		
Rentals of halls, and stage expense	166,873		
Advertising, ticket selling, etc.	118,847		
Office salaries	79,823		
Office rent and other administrative	83,444		
Pensions, social security, etc.	122,631		
Music	25,711		
Membership campaign expense	19,177		
Miscellaneous	54,476	2,423,033	
Academy expense:			
Wages and operating expense	$ 260,412		
Major repairs	41,800		
Interest and depreciation	30,810	333,022	
GROSS EXPENSE			2,756,055
(DEFICIT) FROM OPERATIONS			$ (615,632)
Non-operating income:			
Income from Endowment Funds	$ 189,851		
Campaign contributions	231,354	421,205	
NET INCOME (LOSS)			$ (194,427)

TABLE II–4—Cont.

The Philadelphia Orchestra Association
and
Academy of Music of Philadelphia, Inc.

STATEMENT OF CONSOLIDATED ASSETS AND LIABILITIES
August 31, 1967

ASSETS

General Fund:

Cash ($100,070 restricted)	$ 417,451
U. S. Treasury Bills, at cost (market value $198,113)	196,226
Academy Restoration Fund, cash and receivables, net of $18,040 deferred income	207,811
Notes and accounts receivable	349,910
Prepaid expenses	64,096
Academy of Music (land at cost, building at stated value of $1)	629,611
Deferred expense—challenge program	59,248
Total—General Fund	$1,924,353

Trust Funds (Cash and Investments):

Endowment Fund, restricted (market value $3,557,297)	2,712,128
Endowment Fund, unrestricted (market value $932,302)	950,590
	$5,587,071

LIABILITIES AND FUNDS PRINCIPAL

General Fund:

Accounts payable and accrued expenses		$ 485,144
Special purpose fund—challenge program:		
Total contributions received	$187,797	
Less: Air conditioning expenses	106,870	80,927
Special purpose funds—Academy Restoration Fund		207,811
Special purpose funds—other		19,143
Long-term debt—4% mortgage payable to The Philadelphia Orchestra Association Endowment Fund, maturity 1976		322,710
Deferred income, applicable to 1967–68 season		715,206
Reserve for severance fees		75,000
Unappropriated funds		18,412
Total—General Fund		$1,924,353

Trust Funds—Principal:

Endowment Fund, restricted	2,712,128
Endowment Fund, unrestricted	950,590
	$5,587,071

The Philadelphia Orchestra Association
and
Academy of Music of Philadelphia, Inc.

STATEMENT OF UNAPPROPRIATED FUNDS
September 1, 1966 to August 31, 1967

Balance, September 1, 1966:		
Prior to restatement	$175,339	
Adjustment—royalties accrued as of September 1, 1966	37,500	$ 212,839
Net income (loss) for year ended August 31, 1967		(194,427)
Balance, August 31, 1967		$ 18,412

TABLE II–4—Cont.

ACCOUNTANTS' REPORT

In our opinion, the statement of consolidated assets and liabilities and the related statements of consolidated income and unappropriated funds of The Philadelphia Orchestra Association and Academy of Music of Philadelphia, Inc. present fairly the financial position at August 31, 1967, and the results of their operations for the year then ended. Improvements and Academy of Music restoration costs have not been capitalized pursuant to the established practice of the Academy of Music of Philadelphia, Inc.

Philadelphia, Pennsylvania
October 3, 1967

Main Lafrentz & Co.
Certified Public Accountants

TABLE II–5

THE PHILADELPHIA ORCHESTRA ASSOCIATION
ANNUAL REPORT 1967–68

The Philadelphia Orchestra Association
and
Academy of Music of Philadelphia, Inc.

STATEMENT OF CONSOLIDATED INCOME
Year Ended August 31, 1968

Orchestra income:

Concert income		$1,941,683	
Record royalties		272,438	
Television		5,079	
Commercial sponsorship		17,000	
Miscellaneous		6,913	$2,243,113
Academy income:			
Rentals		$ 196,550	
Other		21,835	218,385
GROSS INCOME			2,461,498
Orchestra expenses:			
Musicians, conductors, soloists		$1,820,236	
Transportation and baggage		93,605	
Musicians' travel allowance		152,545	
Rentals of halls, and stage expense		104,649	
Advertising, ticket selling, etc.		139,821	
Office salaries		84,273	
Office rent and other administrative		60,641	
Pension, social security, etc.		129,747	
Music		27,230	
Miscellaneous		45,712	2,658,459
Academy expense:			
Wages and operating expense		$ 292,169	
Major repairs		42,969	
Interest		12,191	347,329
GROSS EXPENSE			3,005,788
(DEFICIT) FROM OPERATIONS			$ (544,290)
Non-operating income:			
Income from Endowment Funds		$ 208,590	
Campaign contributions, net of campaign expenses—$25,826		231,873	
Ford Foundation contribution, net of Challenge Program expenses—$167,496		26,864	467,327
NET INCOME (LOSS)			$ (76,963)

TABLE II-5—Cont.

The Philadelphia Orchestra Association
and
Academy of Music of Philadelphia, Inc.

CONSOLIDATED BALANCE SHEET
August 31, 1968

ASSETS
General Fund:

Cash, including $300,934 interest bearing	$ 836,771
Cash, restricted funds, including $60,000 interest bearing	141,694
Academy Restoration Fund	29,647
Notes and accounts receivable	216,863
Prepaid expenses	60,721
Academy of Music (land at cost, building at stated value of $1)	629,611
Total—General Fund	$1,915,307

Endowment Trust Funds (Cash and Investments):

Restricted (market value $3,582,895)	2,684,058
Unrestricted (market value $948,639)	945,378
Challenge Program, restricted (market value $545,690)	534,425
	$6,079,168

LIABILITIES AND FUNDS PRINCIPAL
General Fund:

Accounts payable and accrued expenses		$ 638,375
Special purpose funds:		
Challenge Program:		
Total contributions received	$1,457,185	
(Less): Air conditioning expenditures	(794,088)	
Transfers to Endowment Fund	(534,425)	128,672
Academy Restoration Fund		29,647
Other		13,022
Long-term debt—4% mortgage payable to The Philadelphia Orchestra Association Endowment Fund, maturity 1976		298,701
Deferred income, applicable to 1968–69 season		788,641
Reserve for severance fees		76,800
Unappropriated funds (deficit)		(58,551)
Total—General Fund		$1,915,307

Endowment Trust Funds—Principal:

Restricted	2,684,058
Unrestricted	945,378
Challenge Program, restricted	534,425
	$6,079,168

The Philadelphia Orchestra Association
and
Academy of Music of Philadelphia, Inc.

STATEMENT OF UNAPPROPRIATED FUNDS
Year Ended August 31, 1968

Balance, September 1, 1967	$ 18,412
Net income (loss) for year ended August 31, 1968	(76,963)
Balance (deficit), August 31, 1968	$ (58,551)

TABLE II–5—Cont.

STATEMENT OF ACADEMY RESTORATION FUND INCOME AND PRINCIPAL BALANCE
Year Ended August 31, 1968

Total income		$ 300,038
Expenses		108,693
		$ 191,345
Expenditures:		
Improvements and other current expenditures for restoration of Academy of Music	$ 28,718	
Air conditioning	340,792	(369,510)
		$ (178,165)
Principal balance:		
September 1, 1967		207,812
August 31, 1968		$ 29,647

ACCOUNTANTS' REPORT

In our opinion, the consolidated balance sheet and the related statements of income and unappropriated funds of The Philadelphia Orchestra Association and Academy of Music of Philadelphia, Inc. and statement of Academy Restoration Fund income and principal balance present fairly the financial position at August 31, 1968, and the results of their operations for the year then ended. Improvements and Academy of Music restoration costs have not been capitalized pursuant to the established practice of the Academy of Music of Philadelphia, Inc.

Main Lafrentz & Co.

Philadelphia, Pennsylvania
October 7, 1968

CONCLUSION

The Philadelphia Orchestra has survived the loss of the charismatic leader and the large individual contributor, the depression of 1929, the dislocations and turbulence of World War II, and the postwar inflationary period. Moreover, as a non-profit organization, its financial position today is comparatively strong. It has accomplished this by maintaining professional excellence and by bureaucratization, that is, by successfully emulating astute business practices of economy and efficiency.

These practices, however, have exacted a high toll: the artistic quality of the Orchestra's programming and the education of its audiences have suffered; it has neglected a responsibility to American culture by largely ignoring modern music and catering instead to the conservative musical tastes of its upper class audience; the spectrum of concert artists presented has been restricted; its musicians have been exploited in various ways with a resultant lowering of morale and worsening of labor relations; and, finally, it has neglected the musical education of the young and served the cultural needs of only a small and narrow segment of the community. This study will demonstrate later that these costs are now threatening to destroy the organization.

Yet, given the conditions which they have faced, the Directors have not had a wide choice of alternatives for preserving the institution. Cultural non-profit organizations lead, at best, a precarious existence under a private economy. Regardless of its proclaimed goals of artistic and social service, the alternatives of the Philadelphia Orchestra Association have been restricted by the economic realities of a system which leaves such organizations to fend for themselves. The long-held belief that cultural organizations in the United States are able to pursue their artistic and social goals free of interference or dictation is false. The truth is that the restrictions which our market economy places upon such organizations as the price of their survival are as real as the decrees promulgated by any authoritarian government. The freedom of such organizations has always been largely illusory. It is, in fact, the same freedom of dubious value once "enjoyed" by the working classes before labor relations was considered to be properly within the purview of governmental concern; namely, the freedom to starve.

If we understand this, we can address ourselves to the question of large government subsidy at a later point in this study with less trepidation about interference with the liberties of cultural organizations and a more constructive concern with how government subsidy might be used to free such organizations from the grip of the market economy and bureaucratization to better pursue goals of artistic and social service.

At this point the question arises as to whether, even under our system, it has been necessary for the Philadelphia Orchestra to bureaucratize to the extent which it has. In other words, are there reasons, beyond mere survival, why the organization has clung so long and tenaciously to the same policies and procedures?

The answer to this question lies in the nature of the leadership, its motivations, and its value structure. The next chapter will proceed to examine these factors.

Chapter III

The Leadership

The Social Character of the Board of Directors

From political theory we learn that, among the values for which men compete, a high priority is given to prestige, recognition, and status.[1] One place in which these influential values are to be found is within the leadership of cultural organizations. It has been shown that in American cities these positions have been traditionally occupied by and associated with the social elites of the community.[2] Philadelphia has been no exception in this respect.[3] Among the cultural institutions of Philadelphia, the Philadelphia Orchestra has been from its inception a leading index of upper class membership, social recognition, and exclusivity.[4] Leadership in this institution has represented a sought after social commodity. It has even greater value in the particular case of Philadelphia because, as Baltzell has pointed out, social connections are more important in this city than elsewhere in America.[5]

The Philadelphia upper class has been characterized as a white, Anglo-Saxon, Protestant (WASP) group of old hereditary wealth and power.[6] It constitutes a number of families who trace their descent from successful founders of one or more generations ago. Digby Baltzell has described them as follows:

> [They are] at the top of the social class hierarchy; they are brought up together, are friends, and are intermarried one with another; and finally they maintain a distinctive style of life and a kind of primary group solidarity which sets them apart from the rest of the population. As Dixon Whecter [sic] put it: "a group of families with a common background and racial origin becomes cohesive, and fortifies itself by the joint sharing of sports and social activities, by friendship and intermarriage."[7]

The Philadelphia upper class experiences common neighborhoods, common early and higher education, common social activities, and, ultimately, common careers, clubs, and associational memberships.

The result of this total socialization process is a common outlook and shared values. At a later point in this chapter when the attitudes of the leadership toward the Orchestra and its responsibilities are examined, it will be well to remember that these individuals are not only set off from the general population by a distinctive life style, but also by a distinctive value structure.[8]

To trace the predominance of this upper class in the leadership of the Philadelphia Orchestra Association from its founding in 1900 to the present time, the *Social Register of Philadelphia* has been utilized. Such students of the upper class as Domhoff, Baltzell, Wecter, and Amory agree upon the validity of the *Social Register* as the best guide to upper class identification.[9] Registration is based upon a difficult application ritual and a rigid constellation of racial, religious, social, professional, residential, reputational, and lineal requirements which insure the utmost exclusivity. The publication dates from 1888, and it has been said of it: "America's associational aristocracy was born with the advent of the *Social Register.*"[10]

The following three tables contain the names of Board members of the Philadelphia Orchestra Association: Table III–1 lists the founding Boarding members; Table III–2 contains all Board members from incorporation in 1901 to 1969, with length of service; and Table III–3 designates all Presidents and Chairmen of the Board, with length of service. The last list is a particularly significant clue to organizational control inasmuch as there is evidence to indicate that the Association has essentially been a series of one- or two-man operations, with power emanating from these offices.[11] In all the Tables, the designation (SR) is used to indicate *Social Register* listing; and, in Tables III–2 and III–3, the asterisk (*) identifies those members who currently serve on the Board.

TABLE III–1

FOUNDING BOARD MEMBERS OF THE PHILADELPHIA
ORCHESTRA ASSOCIATION

George Burnham, Jr.		Edward G. McCollin	
A. J. Cassatt	(SR)[a]	Thomas McKean	(SR)
John H. Converse	(SR)	Clement B. Newbold	(SR)
Eckley B. Coxe, Jr.	(SR)	James W. Paul, Jr.	(SR)
William L. Elkins	(SR)	Mrs. Frank H. Rosengarten	(SR)
Miss Mary K. Gibson	(SR)	Richard Rossmassler	
Clement A. Griscom	(SR)	Edgar Scott	(SR)
Mrs. Alfred C. Harrison	(SR)	Simon A. Stern	
John H. Ingham	(SR)	Miss Anne Thomson	(SR)
Oliver B. Judson	(SR)	Alexander Van Rensselaer	(SR)
Edward I. Keffer		Henry Whelen, Jr.	(SR)
C. Hartman Kuhn	(SR)	P. A. B. Widener	(SR)

[a](SR) designates *Social Register* listing.

SOURCE: Frances Anne Wister, *Twenty-Five Years of the Philadelphia Orchestra* (Philadelphia: Philadelphia Women's Committees for the Philadelphia Orchestra, 1925), p. 25.

TABLE III–2

THE PHILADELPHIA ORCHESTRA ASSOCIATION
MEMBERS OF THE BOARD OF DIRECTORS, 1901–1969[a]

A. J. Cassatt	1901–2 to 1905–6 (except for 1904–5)	(SR)[b]
John H. Converse	1901–2 to 1910–11	(SR)
Eckley B. Coxe, Jr.	1901–2 to 1915–16	(SR)
F. T. Sully Darley	1901–2	(SR)
William L. Elkins	1901–2 to 1902–3	(SR)
Miss Mary K. Gibson	1901–2 to 1917–18	(SR)
Clement A. Griscom	1901–2 to 1912–13	(SR)
Mrs. Alfred C. Harrison	1901–2 to 1902–3	(SR)
John H. Ingham	1901–2 to 1930–31	(SR)
Oliver B. Judson	1901–2 to 1904–5	(SR)
Edward I. Keffer	1901–2 to 1907–8	
Oscar A. Knipe	1901–2	
C. Hartman Kuhn	1901–2 to 1933–34	(SR)
Edward G. McCollin	1901–2 to 1907–8	
Thomas McKean, Jr.	1901–2 to 1914–15	(SR)
Clement B. Newbold	1901–2 to 1913–14	(SR)
James W. Paul, Jr.	1901–2 to 1907–8	(SR)
Mrs. Frank H. Rosengarten	1901–2 to 1912–13	(SR)
Edgar Scott	1901–2 to 1913–14	(SR)
Simon A. Stern	1901–2 to 1903–4	
Miss Anne Thomson	1901–2 to 1910–11	(SR)
Alexander Van Rensselaer	1901–2 to 1932–33	(SR)
Henry Whelen, Jr.	1901–2 to 1906–7	(SR)
P. A. B. Widener	1901–2 to 1903–4 and 1905–6 to 1907–8	(SR)
George Burnham, Jr.	1902–3 to 1909–10	
Mrs. William W. Arnett	1903–4 and 1905–6 to 1934–35	(SR)
Richard Rossmassler	1903–4 to 1904–5	
Andrew Wheeler, Jr.	1903–4 to 1926–27	(SR)
Richard Y. Cook	1905–6 to 1916–17	(SR)
Mrs. A. J. Dallas Dixon	1905–6 to 1916–17 and 1918–19 to 1924–25	(SR)
Miss Francis A. Wister	1905–6 to 1955–56	(SR)
E. T. Stotesbury	1907–8 to 1919–20	(SR)
Charles A. Braun	1908–9 to 1921–22	
G. Heide Norris	1908–9 to 1925–26	(SR)
Theodore N. Ely	1909–10 to 1915–16	(SR)
James Crosby Brown	1909–10 to 1929–30	(SR)
Arthur E. Newbold	1907–8 to 1917–18	(SR)
Mrs. L. Howard Weatherly	1911–12 to 1934–35	(SR)
J. R. Barton Willing	1911-12 to 1912–13	(SR)
John F. Braun	1913–14 to 1934–35	
Cyrus H. K. Curtis	1913–14 to 1932–33	

TABLE III–2—Cont.

Mrs. Harold E. Yarnall	1912–13 to 1937–38	(SR)
Edward Bok	1914–15 to 1929–30	
Charles D. Hart	1916–17 to 1933–34	(SR)
Henry McKean Ingersoll	1915–16 to 1934–35	(SR)
Charlton Yarnall	1916–17 to 1934–35	(SR)
Samuel S. Fels	1915–16 to 1934–35	
Effingham B. Morris	1917–18 to 1934–35	(SR)
Joseph E. Widener	1916–17 to 1934–35	(SR)
William J. Turner	1919–20 to 1929–30	(SR)
Robert K. Cassatt	1920–21 to 1932–33	(SR)
Evan Randolph	1922–23 to 1929–30	(SR)
Effingham B. Morris, Jr.	1916–17 to 1934–35	(SR)
William Phillip Barba	1926–27 to 1932–33	
Owen J. Roberts	1926–27 to 1929–30	(SR)
Samuel R. Rosenbaum	1928–29 to 1965–66	
William Curtis Bok	1930–31 to 1934–35	
Henry G. Brengle	1930–31 to 1934–35	(SR)
Arthur Judson	1931–32 to 1934–35	
Herbert J. Yily	1931–32 to 1932–33	
Charles G. Berwind[c]	1933–34 to 1968–69	(SR)
Orville H. Bullitt[c]	1933–34 to 1968–69	(SR)
Alfred Reginald Allen	1933–34 to 1935–36	(SR)
Benjamin H. Ludlow	1933–34 to 1945–46	
Charles Edwin Fox	1934–35 to 1936–37	
John E. Zimmerman	1934–35	(SR)
G. Ruhland Rebmann, Jr.[c]	1934–35 to 1968–69	(SR)
Harl McDonald	1935–36 to 1954–55	
Phillip C. Staples	1935–36 to 1948–49	(SR)
Thomas S. Gates	1935–36 to 1947–48	(SR)
J. Stogdell Stokes	1935–36 to 1947–48	(SR)
Eugene V. Alessandroni	1935–36 to 1959–60	
Miss Mary Stewart Hodge	1935–36	(SR)
C. David Hocker	1936–37 to 1937–38	
William Fulton Kurtz	1937–38 to 1962–63	(SR)
Curtin Winsor[c]	1938–39 to 1968–69	(SR)
W. Logan MacCoy	1938–39 to 1946–47	(SR)
Lessing J. Rosenwald[c]	1938–39 to 1968–69	
Harry A. Batten	1938–39 to 1965–66	
H. Tatnall Brown, Jr.	1938–39 to 1946–47	(SR)
John C. Harvey	1938–39 to 1941–42	
R. Sturgis Ingersoll	1938–39 to 1967–68	(SR)
Mrs. Nathan Hayward	1939–40 to 1951–52	(SR)
Mrs. Wharton Sinkler	1939–40 to 1952–53	(SR)
Henry P. McIlhenny[c]	1939–40 to 1968–69	(SR)
John A. Davis, Jr.	1943–44	
George T. Eager	1944–45 to 1949–50	
John B. Thayer	1944–45 to 1945–46	(SR)

TABLE III–2—Cont.

Mrs. Herbert C. Morris[c]	1945–46 to 1968–69	(SR)
Henry Clifford[c]	1946–47 to 1968–69	(SR)
Arthur Littleton	1946–47 to 1953–54	(SR)
Mrs. Emile C. Geyelin[c]	1947–48 to 1968–69	(SR)
C. Alison Scully	1947–48 to 1954–55	(SR)
E. A. Roberts	1948–49 to 1959–60	(SR)
S. S. Neuman	1949–50 to 1957–58	
Frederick D. Garman	1950–51 to 1951–52	
Bernard Samuel	1950–51 to 1951–52	
C. Wanton Balis, Jr.[c]	1951–52 to 1968–69	(SR)
Crawford H. Greenewalt[c]	1953–54 to 1968–69	(SR)
Mrs. James S. Hatfield, Jr.[c]	1953–54 to 1968–69	(SR)
J. Kent Willing, Jr.	1953–54 to 1954–55	(SR)
James A. Finnegan	1953–54 to 1954–55	
Frederick R. Mann	1953–54 to 1956–57	
Roger S. Firestone[c]	1955–56 to 1968–69	(SR)
Victor E. Moore	1953–54 to 1956–67	
J. Peter Williams[c]	1955–56 to 1968–69	(SR)
Stuart F. Loucheim[c]	1957–58 to 1968–69	
Wilfred D. Gillen	1958–59 to 1967–68	
Matthew H. McCloskey	1958–59 to 1964–65	
J. Tyson Stokes[c]	1957–58 to 1968–69	(SR)
Bernard L. Frankel[c]	1960–61 to 1968–69	
Henry W. Sawyer, III[c]	1960–61 to 1968–69	(SR)
Harry R. Neilson, Jr.[c]	1963–64 to 1968–69	(SR)
Hugh K. Duffield	1965–66 to 1967–68	
Richard C. Bond[c]	1966–67 to 1968–69	(SR)
Fred E. Braemer[c]	1966–67 to 1968–69	
Morris Duane[c]	1966–67 to 1968–69	(SR)
Robert O. Fickes[c]	1966–67 to 1968–69	(SR)
William S. Fishman[c]	1966–67 to 1968–69	
Robert F. Gilkeson[c]	1966–67 to 1968–69	
Charles A. Meyer	1966–67 to 1967–68	
Stuart T. Saunders[c]	1966–67 to 1968–69	(SR)
Mrs. Frederick T. van Urk[c]	1966–67 to 1968–69	
Gustave G. Amsterdam[c]	1968–69	
James F. Bodine[c]	1968–69	(SR)
H. Gates Lloyd, III[c]	1968–69	(SR)
Robert Montgomery Scott[c]	1968–69	(SR)

Total service of Directors listed in the *Social Register of Philadelphia* = 1,175 years.
Total service of other Directors = 390 years.

[a]All seasons listed are inclusive.

[b](SR) designates *Social Register* listing.

[c]Denotes present Board membership.

SOURCE: Philadelphia Orchestra programs.

TABLE III–3

THE PHILADELPHIA ORCHESTRA ASSOCIATION
PRESIDENTS AND CHAIRMEN OF THE BOARD
1901–1969

Alexander Van Rensselaer, President	1901–2 to 1932–33	(SR)[a]
Curtis Bok, President	1934–35	
Thomas S. Gates, President	1935–36 to 1937–38	(SR)
Chairman of the Board	1938–39 to 1947–48	
Orville H. Bullitt, President	1938–39 to 1954–55	(SR)
Chairman of the Board	1955–56 to 1966–67	
C. Wanton Balis, Jr., President	1955–56 to 1968–69	(SR)
Chairman of the Board[b]	1968–69	
Richard C. Bond, President[b]	1968–69	(SR)

[a](SR) denotes *Social Register* listing.
[b]Denotes present incumbent.
SOURCE: Philadelphia Orchestra programs.

Table III–1 reveals that, of the 24 founders of the Philadelphia Orchestra Association, 19 were listed in the *Social Register of Philadelphia*. Table III–2 shows that, of the 128 individuals who have served as Directors, 84 have been listed in the *Register*—indicating that they have been almost twice as numerous as those who did not come from this social grouping. Table III–2 also shows that the Directors who have had listing in the *Register* have served a total of 1,175 years compared to a total of 390 years for the others. Their total tenure, in short, has been almost triple that of those Directors who did not belong to this elite group. Finally, Table III–3 reveals that, with the exception of one year, there never has been, in the history of the Philadelphia Orchestra Association, a President or Chairman of the Board who was not a member of the *Register*.

THE IMPACT OF THE FORD FOUNDATION GRANT
UPON THE COMPOSITION OF THE BOARD

In 1966, the Ford Foundation made a grant of two million dollars to the Philadelphia Orchestra Association with a proviso that four million dollars in matching funds be raised by the organization prior to June 30, 1971.[12]

Shortly thereafter, Hugh Duffield, a retired businessman who was not a member of the *Register* but possessed an outstanding record of public service and a reputation for being able to get things done, was elected to Board membership and named Chairman of the four million dollar fund drive.[13] In addition, a professional firm was retained to manage the drive.

After a preliminary investigation, the consulting firm issued a report which urged that, among other things, the Association broaden its base of support in the community and better its image by adding 12 new Directors to the Board who would represent "leading business, religious, ethnic, etc., segments of the current Philadelphia sociological structure—to counter charges that the Board is WASP-oriented [White–Anglo-Saxon–Protestant].[14] Duffield, newly-elected Chairman of the fund drive, followed this report by a public statement to the effect that the Orchestra "belongs to the people of Philadelphia and that the new Directors should represent the community."[15]

The Board responded to the report to the extent of amending the by-laws of the Association to permit the addition of 12 new Directors.[16] It soon became evident, however, that the Board was not about to yield on the issue of community representation. Board spokesmen, in announcing plans to add the new Directors, pointedly observed that the move was not aimed at softening any criticism of lack of community representation. The President of the Association declared: "Enlarging the Board has not been undertaken to include any particular ethnic or racial groups—our aim is to get people who can help us to raise money."[17] He went on to make it clear that the new Directors would be drawn mainly from the business community.[18]

At the present time, in spite of the pressures for opening

up the leadership which were generated by the Ford Foundation grant, all indications are that the Board has continued to resist community representation. This is illustrated by Table III–4, which gives the present Board membership, *Social Register* listing, and professional or business association. Of a total of 33 Directors, 24 are listed in the *Register*, thus according an even higher percentage of representation to this group than it enjoyed in 1965 prior to the Ford Foundation grant, when there were 17 out of 24 similarly listed. Both the new President and the new Chairman of the Board are listed in the *Register*. The domination of the Board by big businessmen and lawyers from successful and prestigious firms identified with corporate practice is overwhelming. There are 22 individuals on the Board associated with large business, including coal, department stores, shipping, insurance, banking, utilities, rubber, chemicals, investments, publishing, and railroads. Of the seven lawyers, six are associated with firms designated by the Placement Office of the University of Pennsylvania Law School as among the most successful and prestigious in Philadelphia, and all engage in corporate and banking practice. The remainder of the Board consists of two wealthy philanthropists, one architect, and one individual who heads an organization that acts as an advocate for the private enterprise system. No representation has been accorded to Negroes, professional musicians, city government, organized labor, educators, or other significant community elements. Some representation has been accorded to the Jewish community in the persons of Lessing J. Rosenwald, Bernard L. Frankel, Fred E. Braemer, William S. Fishman, Gustave G. Amsterdam, and the wife of Walter H. Annenberg. However, these individuals are drawn from the uppermost economic strata of the Jewish community and in actuality belong to the same business elite grouping as the other Board members.

TABLE III–4

PHILADELPHIA ORCHESTRA ASSOCIATION
BOARD OF DIRECTORS, 1968–69

Name	*Social Register*	*Professional or Business Association (or that of spouse)*
Charles G. Berwind	yes	Chairman, Berwind Corp.
Orville H. Bullitt	yes	President, Beaver Coal Co.
G. Ruhland Rebmann, Jr.	yes	Law, Obermayer, Rebmann, Maxwell & Hippel
Curtin Winsor	yes	Executive Director, Americans for the Competitive Enterprise System
Lessing J. Rosenwald	no	Chairman, Sears Roebuck Co. (retired)
Henry P. McIlhenny	yes	Retired Philanthropist
Mrs. Herbert C. Morris	yes	Tasty Baking Co.
Henry Clifford	yes	Retired Philanthropist
Mrs. Emile C. Geyelin	yes	President, French Line (deceased)
C. Wanton Balis, Jr. (Chairman of the Board)	yes	President, Balis & Co.
Crawford H. Greenewalt	yes	Chairman of the Finance Committee, E. I. du Pont de Nemours & Co.
Mrs. James S. Hatfield, Jr.	yes	Architect
Roger S. Firestone	yes	Director, Firestone Tire and Rubber Co.
J. Peter Williams	yes	Law, Drinker, Biddle & Reath
Stuart F. Loucheim	no	Distributor, Electronic & Sound Equipment
J. Tyson Stokes	yes	Law, Morgan, Lewis & Bockius
Bernard L. Frankel	no	Law, Fox, Rothschild, O'Brien & Frankel
Henry W. Sawyer, III	yes	Law, Drinker, Biddle & Reath
Harry R. Neilson, Jr.	yes	Newburger & Co.
Richard C. Bond (President)	yes	Chairman and Chief Executive Officer, John Wanamaker
Fred E. Braemer	no	Chairman, Globe Protection Co.
Morris Duane	yes	Law, Duane, Morris & Heckscher
Robert O. Fickes	yes	Chairman and President, Philco Ford Corp.
William S. Fishman	no	President, Automatic Retailers of America

TABLE III–4—Cont.

Name	Social Register	Professional or Business Association (or that of spouse)
Robert F. Gilkeson	no	President, Philadelphia Electric Co.
Stuart T. Saunders	yes	Chairman and Chief Executive Officer, Penn Central Co.
Mrs. Frederick T. van Urk	no	F. T. van Urk Insurance Agency
Gustave G. Amsterdam	no	Chairman and President, Bankers Securities Corp.
James F. Bodine	yes	Senior Vice-President, First Pennsylvania Banking & Trust Co.
H. Gates Lloyd, III	yes	Vice-President, Drexel, Harriman, Ripley, Inc.
Robert Montgomery Scott	yes	Law, Montgomery, McCracken, Walker & Rhoads
Mrs. Walter H. Annenberg	no	Publisher, *Philadelphia Inquirer*
Mrs. Charles E. Mather, 2nd	yes	President, Mather & Co.

SOURCES: *Poor's Register of Corporation Directors and Executives, 1969.*
Martindale-Hubbell Law Directory, 1969.
Philadelphia Orchestra programs.

From all the above, it is clear that the Ford Foundation grant has had little effect upon the social character of the Board of Directors, which remains an index of prestige and social status. Its exclusive character has been preserved.

THE ORIENTATION OF THE BOARD OF DIRECTORS

In determining how the present Directors view the Philadelphia Orchestra and its responsibilities, the author has held discussions with Board members, present and former Orchestra members, professional staff of the Association, local individuals active in musical affairs, labor mediators, labor lawyers, union officials, city government representatives, and other individuals who have had personal contact with the Orchestra leadership in the context of Association affairs.

Material from a professional evaluation commissioned by the Association itself in 1967 has also been utilized to furnish confirmation of the Board's attitudes as reported herein.[19] This latter study conducted confidential interviews with a selected sampling of leading Philadelphians, including 13 Directors of the Association, staff members, Orchestra members, and a number of persons knowledgeable in the fields of philanthropy, music, and civic affairs. At the same time, as part of the same study, an institutional questionnaire was completed by the Association and analyzed by a professional staff.

The orientation of the Board of Directors may be determined by the answers to the following three questions:

(1) Do the Directors feel that there should be community representation on the Board of the Philadelphia Orchestra? If not, how is this rationalized?

(2) Do the Directors feel that the Orchestra has any responsibility to advance the art of symphonic music by playing modern music?

(3) Do the Directors feel that the organization has any responsibility for serving all segments of the community?

In regard to the first question, not one Board member, as far as it has been possible to determine, advocates community representation. A long-term Director spoke for most of those in the *Social Register* when he declared: "Look, this organization belongs to the Main Line because that kind of person started it and that kind of person has kept it alive. We're the people who care for and appreciate the Orchestra. If you let every Tom, Dick, and Harry on the Board this institution will go down the drain." Another Board member summed up the feeling of the others, who are not in the

Social Register but oppose community representation on other grounds: "We don't need Negroes, educators, or musicians on the Board because they don't swing any financial weight. We need people who can pull in big money."

C. Wanton Balis, Jr., former President of the Association and present Chairman of the Board, spoke for a majority of the Directors when he declared that the Orchestra owed its existence, and therefore its allegiance, to the small group of people who appreciated it and had been willing to show that appreciation in the past by working for the organization, attending concerts, and contributing financially to it. (This, in effect, means a small elite since they are, for the most part, the only ones who have either been invited into the organization or, as will be later shown, approached for financial support.)

The professional survey commissioned by the Association revealed a public awareness of this attitude, as expressed by Mr. Balis. Its report stated:

> There exists a considerable body of *opinion* among sources both internal and external to the Philadelphia Orchestra Association that the Association, often referred to as the "Establishment," has traditionally been a closed corporation, governed by "the dictate of a few within a few." These same sources feel that the Association has been run with the sole purpose in mind of serving to enrich the lives of and satisfy the needs of a small body of acceptable persons to whom it is considered that the Orchestra "really belongs."[20]

This outlook of the Board is buttressed by two rationales. First, the Philadelphia Orchestra has traditionally been an upper class institution toward which its aristocratic leaders have felt a strong sense of *noblesse oblige*.[21] The persistence of this attiude and the determination to preserve this prestigious class ownership remains strong within a group which is still noted for its dedication to maintaining the traditional aspects of Philadelphia life.²² It finds expression, for example, in the outspoken antipathy which some Board members display toward those whom they characterize as "pushy" individuals with "brash new money." This is illustrated by the case of Frederick R. Mann, a prominent Jewish business-man who made his fortune in the paper box industry after World War II. Mann, as City Representative, secured a seat on the Board of the Association in 1953 by virtue of an annual grant to the Orchestra of $50,000 from City Council. After three seasons, the Board removed Mann and notified the city that they would forego the appropriation. One Board member confided: "Fred's aggressiveness and outspoken ways offended the Board. He wasn't satisfied to just sit on the Board. He wanted to know about everything that was going on, and he took to calling the office and making sug-gestions to the manager. The Board was afraid that he was trying to take over."

The Mann episode points out an interesting paradox. A majority of the Board were businessmen and oriented toward economic considerations. Mann had demonstrated his ability to raise large sums of money, not only from the city, but also, in his capacity as President of Robin Hood Dell, from the Jewish community of Philadelphia. Yet, no amount of financial incentive could bring the Board to retain an indi-vidual whom they perceived as a threat to their upper class control of the organization.

The same paradox is evident in the Board's continuing insistence upon maintaining a certain amount of exclusivity. It will not take money from just anyone if it means granting Board representation to individuals who might alter its public image of a social and financial elite. For example, when the author conveyed an offer of a large annual contri-bution in 1963 from one of the major labor unions in Phila-delphia in exchange for a seat on the Board, it evoked no response from the Association. Again, when the author, in 1968, conveyed an offer of substantial assistance from the city in exchange for a seat on the Board for the City Representative (no longer Frederick R. Mann), the lack of interest on the part of the Association was rationalized by one Board member as follows: "Dealing with the city is just a big headache. If we take money from them they'll want the Orchestra to play at the baseball games." This was an obvious evasion since the City Representative had attached no stipulations to the offer. To the Board, although principally businessmen, an elite image is apparently more important than financial gain for the organization.

The second rationale underlying the Board's outlook is an attitude common to many individuals who work without monetary compensation in the leadership of non-profit organizations. This might, for want of a better appellation, be called the non-profit syndrome.[23] These people view themselves as the "winter soldiers" who have tended the flame throughout long periods of adversity and public apathy. They acquire a vested emotional interest in the organization which expresses itself as some undefined right of possession. This is manifested by Directors of the Philadelphia Orchestra whenever the suggestion is made that the composition of the Board be altered. They point heatedly to the long hours and hard work which they and their friends have given without compensation in the service of the Orchestra. This same rationale is advanced in labor relations when the Directors indignantly deny that the Orchestra members are exploited or have any special claims beyond mere employees upon the organization.[24]

In regard to the second question concerning the viewpoint of the Board on the responsibility of the organization for the advancement of symphonic music, by playing modern works, there is little evidence which has come to light to indicate any understanding or interest on the part of the Directors in granting exposure to representative contemporary works, in experimenting with new concert formats, or in varying the concert programs.[25] Without exception, every Board member interviewed felt that the artistic obligation of the Philadelphia Orchestra was simply to maintain a high level of excellence in performance. On the question of programming, most Board members admit to being laymen with at best a rudimentary knowledge of music. There are no practicing professional musicians on the Board. Most express a dislike of modern music and a partiality toward the traditional in programming, but add that they consider this area to be the sole prerogative of the Musical Director. Significantly enough, however, many declared that if his programming or choice of soloists were to provoke adverse audience reaction at the box office, this would rightly become a concern of the Board. The leading Board members who are businessmen were particularly frank in making it clear that the material interests of the organization took precedence over experimentation or innovation. The Musical Director, of course, is well aware of both the concern for the sale of tickets and the musical preferences of those who hire him. The result is that the advancement of symphonic music, in the terms set forth above, does not enjoy a high organizational priority because, among other reasons, it is not accorded much importance in the value structure of the Directors.

The third question concerns the viewpoint of the Directors toward the responsibilities of the organization for serving the community. The majority of the Board feel strongly that only a relative few are capable of appreciating the great music and the high quality product which the Philadelphia Orchestra offers. This was summarized by one Board member who declared: "This talk of playing for more people in the community is nonsense. Let's face it, most of the people in this town aren't interested in hearing your kind of music, let alone being able to appreciate how well you fellows play it." The Board is also opposed to a wider variety of activities calculated to involve the organization with greater numbers in the community because, in addition to its not being lucrative, the Board feels that, whenever the Orchestra does not play a specific type of music in the traditional manner at the Academy of Music, it cheapens itself. One leading official was adamant on this point when he said: "I'll resign before I permit you fellows to play a bunch of junk all over town. We'd have to be pretty desperate before we'd stoop to making a circus out of this institution."

The sense of *noblesse oblige* and the personal value structures of the Board do not tend toward community service in the wide sense, but manifest themselves as a felt responsibility toward a small group of patrons and a sanctified institutional aura which has been traditionally associated with their own class. For example, although the open air concerts at the Robin Hood Dell in Fairmount Park have historically been the only means by which many thousands of citizens and young people can hear the Orchestra at little or no cost, the Board never assumed any responsibility for these concerts, which had no official connection with the Philadelphia Orchestra Association, until they were compelled to very recently. Robin Hood Dell Concerts, Inc., is an autonomous organization, under an entirely different leadership, drawn from another social segment of the population. At one time the musicians of the Orchestra kept these concerts alive by running them on a cooperative basis for very little income. In 1948, when they failed for lack of funds, the Philadelphia Orchestra Association made no move to continue them. Only the intervention of a group headed by Frederick R. Mann enabled the Dell to survive.

Another example of the Board's attitude toward community service is its expressed distaste for proposals that the Orchestra perform a few concerts of a popular nature at Convention Hall, a municipal facility which can seat many more people than the Academy of Music. The past President of the Association declared that the Orchestra would do this sort of thing if it were forced to, but that it would be a sorry day for the Orchestra to be so degraded. One Board member, who feels differently, complained that he is in a decided minority on this question, and that his attempts so far to interest other Board members in some concerts at Convention Hall have met with no response or outright hostility.

The professional survey conducted for the Association demonstrated that the community is aware of these attitudes and resents them. It reported as follows:

> It is charged that the small self-perpetuating group guiding the affairs of the Orchestra has been unwilling to consider ways and means of sharing the Orchestra or introducing the Orchestra to more segments of the Greater Philadelphia population through more community-type concerts—more youth concerts—and more suburban concerts. It appears that Robinhood [sic] Dell does not fill this need since respondents are quick to point out that this is not *the* Philadelphia Orchestra in concert. The charge continues that the Orchestra management is preoccupied with record sales, in playing for traditional patrons in Philadelphia and touring for sales appeal. The claim is that it is difficult to try to book the Orchestra for other than this. . . . Those voicing this criticism more often than not offer their own remedial action in suggesting that they would like to see the Orchestra introduced to more Philadelphians (including themselves) by more community-type concerts in Convention Hall at popular prices or through suburban concerts in the larger high school auditoriums or through a portable shell as in New York.[26]

At the present time most Board members agree that the Orchestra should be reaching more young people, but feel that these concerts are too costly. There is general agreement that nothing will be done in this area unless outside sources provide the necessary funds. No organizational resources are presently committed for the expansion of this type of activity. A similar pragmatic position concerning the costs involved is evident among the minority of Board members who harbor no personal objections to the Orchestra becoming available to wider segments of the community on a limited basis. If the money were forthcoming, they would be willing to undertake a few activities which would not disrupt the established schedule. In this case also, however, they are unwilling to commit any substantial organizational resources for the purpose. Without exception, the Board members interviewed were proud of the businesslike way in which the Orchestra is run. To them, considerations of economy and efficiency took undisputed preference over any obligations which they may have felt the Orchestra owed to the community at large. It is important to note that most Board members do not deny that the Association could afford to make a limited gesture in the direction of community service, such as a few concerts for young people in the schools or some low-priced concerts at Convention Hall. The overwhelming majority of the Board, however, are businessmen and lawyers and they simply do not see this as an efficient way to run an organization. To these individuals, economy of operation is not something which is forced upon the organization by circumstances, but a desirable end in itself which should be accorded the highest priority. In summation, the concept of making the Orchestra available to more people in the community through a variety of activities is personally distasteful to most Board members and goes against their basic values as businessmen.

The Directors of the Philadelphia Orchestra Association view the responsibilities of the organization toward the community in an entirely different way from that discussed above. Their concept of community service flows from their own distinctive value structure as members of the upper class. Their activities are directed toward serving the interests of that class. For example, the prestigious activities of the Philadelphia Orchestra, such as touring and recording, not only bring renown to the organization, but also serve to enhance the image of the Philadelphia upper class with which it is associated. Similarly, the activities of the Orchestra enhance the city image both nationally and internationally, and this is considered a service to business, tourism, professional recruitment in industry, etc. Thus, the Board helps to further the economic interests of its own class. One Board member declared: "We've done more to put this town on the map than any other outfit around, and the business interests here know it!" Finally, the traditional concert format to which the Orchestra adheres serves the cultural needs of the upper class, and the conservative programming reflects their preferences. In summation, the concept of community service which is held by the Board emerges in practice as service to the social, economic, and cultural interests of the upper class as well as the personal interests, in terms of prestige and status, of the Directors.

The Use of Economy and Efficiency to Maintain Organizational Control

The strategy of the Directors for maintaining organizational control has been to adhere to strict policies of economy and efficiency of operation that keep the annual deficit small enough to be recovered from a relatively few contributors.

This makes it possible to limit organizational support to the same upper class as the leadership and prevent significant penetration of the Board by other social groups through financial means. The Association has declared that its operating deficit is taken care of by "friends" in contrast to the general public,[27] and the upper-class nature of this support is a matter of public record.[28]

Table III–5 lists the annual contributions made to the Philadelphia Orchestra Association and the number of contributors for the seasons 1953–54 through 1967–68. Note that the number of annual contributors has been as low as 1,982 and has never exceeded 3,836. These figures represent a metropolitan area of over three million population which, according to many sources, recognized the value of the Orchestra to the community and would be willing, under the right conditions, to contribute to its support.[29]

TABLE III–5

THE PHILADELPHIA ORCHESTRA ASSOCIATION
CONTRIBUTIONS AND CONTRIBUTORS

Season	Contributions	Number of Contributors
53–54	$106,178.85	2,800
54–55	$116,276.66	2,900
55–56	$131,366.00	2,968
56–67	$118,069.00	2,764
57–58	$129,871.63	2,735
58–59	$130,818.03	2,573
59–60	$134,967.09	2,615
60–61	$137,536.71	2,492
61–62	$127,703.94	1,982
62–63	$179,030.79	3,050
63–64	$203,197.23	3,389
64–65	$211,812.90	3,643
65–66	$237,863.62	3,706
66–67	$231,354.10	3,836
67–68	$261,321.50	3,677

SOURCE: Philadelphia Orchestra Association

Conclusion

The leadership of the Philadelphia Orchestra has been dominated, from its inception and up to and including the present time, by a closed upper-class elite as defined by the *Social Register*. Because leadership of this institution has always been a leading index of upper-class membership, social recognition, and exclusivity, it is a sought-after commodity which brings status and prestige to the individual members of the Board of Directors. Moreover, in addition to realizing these personal benefits, the Directors have utilized the organization to serve the economic and cultural needs of their own class.

At the end of Chapter II the question was posed whether our private economic system was solely accountable for the extent and persistence of bureaucratization in the Philadelphia Orchestra. It has now been shown that part of the responsibility for these policies of extreme economy, efficiency, and routinization lies with the elite leadership, which utilizes them to maintain and perpetuate its control. Because these policies serve successfully to minimize the organizational deficit, they enable the leadership to recoup it each year from a small circle of loyal supporters and thereby resist financial penetration of the Board by other social groups.

The Board members, being mostly businessmen, have also adopted the values of economy and efficiency as overriding organizational goals because these are congenial to their own personal value structures. There is a striking and paradoxical exception here, however. Although the Directors are primarily businessmen, in any situation where considerable financial gain might accrue to the organization at the cost of jeopardizing upper-class control, the class loyalties of the

Directors have taken precedence over their economic values and they have chosen to forego these benefits.

Finally, the costs which have been shown to result from bureaucratization—namely, ultra-conservative programming, restricted community service, and labor alienation—are not regarded as important by a majority of the Board. Ultra-conservative programming suits their own musical preferences; they do not consider that they have any obligation to make the Orchestra available to anyone in the community except a select group; and the members of the Orchestra are not considered to have any significant claims upon the organization.[30]

Chapter IV

Alienation

PART 1—THE NATURE AND CAUSES OF ALIENATION IN THE PHILADELPHIA ORCHESTRA

There is considerable evidence that some members of the Philadelphia Orchestra experience both an alienation from the work which they perform and an alienation from the management of the organization in which they perform it. This chapter will (1) analyze such evidence and (2) show its significance for the Philadelphia Orchestra.

The causes of both types of alienation can be traced to the various aspects of bureaucratization which have been previously set forth in this study. In the case of alienation from management, the causes arise out of management's heavy emphasis upon economy, which has led to bitter feeling and strikes over such issues as wages, pensions, extensive touring, contractual infractions, recording procedures, favoritism, and heavy work schedules.[1] In the case of alienation from the work performed, the cause arises out of the routinization of the traditional symphonic format (employment of the full orchestra in the same traditional works under the sole discretion of a conductor) which blocks the individual's needs for self-expression, recognition, and sustained interest in his work. This is particularly true for Orchestra members who sit within the string sections and have no individual part to perform. Moreover, the constant repetition of repertoire leads to boredom and precludes the involvement of the individual in his work. These factors might not be critical if there were compensatory opportunities on the job for individual recognition and prerogatives. Chamber music performances, solo opportunities, coaching and guidance of students, and small group work in such areas as modern music, education, social welfare, and music therapy are examples of activities which could fill these needs. However, in the Philadelphia Orchestra situation, alienation from work is exacerbated by the repetitious nature of the programs and the unvarying use of the Orchestra in the traditional manner, both of which are endemic to bureaucratization. Routinization and specialization are carried to a point where no other activities are possible within the work situation which might yield some personal satisfaction and recognition for many Orchestra members.

The Move to Year-Round Employment

In early 1963, in a letter to Local 77, American Federation of Musicians, the members of the Philadelphia Orchestra set forth a list of conditions for their upcoming labor contract. They stated: "We are more interested in yearly earnings than in a weekly salary. We believe that the Association should assume responsibility for making us a full-time orchestra."[2] The letter then went on specifically to request that the period of winter employment be extended from 35 to 42 weeks, which, added to a six-week employment period at the Robin Hood Dell during the summer, would constitute a total of 48 weeks of work. It was further requested that the weekly minimum salary be increased from $190.00 to $200.00, and that all Orchestra members with five or more years of service be given two weeks paid vacation.[3] Other sections of the letter dealt with working conditions, job security, and pensions.[4]

At about this same time, the Board was becoming more amenable to making some significant concessions to the musicians in the interests of better labor relations because of certain pressures which were being exerted upon it. For one thing, it was aware of a heightened militancy on the part of the musicians which threatened an escalation of labor conflict. One of the chief disadvantages of the musicians in previous contract negotiations had been the absence of their right to ratify the contract which the union had negotiated in their name. When this concession was obtained from the union shortly before 1963, it meant, in effect, that the musicians could prolong a strike as long as they were dissatisfied with the union's efforts and with what the Association was offering.[5] Another manifestation of the new militancy was the creation by the musicians of a parallel professional organization to the union, the International Conference of Symphony and Opera Musicians (ICSOM). This organization was exerting pressure upon both the union and the employers. In the case of the former, it gave substance to the symphonic musicians' threat to secede from the union and become their own bargaining agents unless the union became more militant. In the case of the employers, ICSOM was formulating new and far-reaching demands to be made of them, such as record royalties for the musicians.[6] However, the single event in this regard which most rudely awakened the Board to what might lie ahead was the demand of the musicians, in April of 1963, for the right, if they so decided, to dismiss the conductor.[7] This move was squelched but it nevertheless shook up the Board.[8] The Directors were strong Ormandy supporters because he had faithfully carried out their policies and because they were well aware of the investment in recordings which he represented.

Another pressure to make economic concessions to the Orchestra members came from the fact that the economic plight of symphonic musicians was coming increasingly to public attention. Hearings on the subject had just taken place before a congressional subcommittee. The findings were being cited to justify a program of federal aid to the arts, a development which the Philadelphia Orchestra Association strongly opposed.[9] In addition, pressure for year-round employment was resulting from the facts that the Boston Symphony Orchestra was fast approaching this objective and that the New York Philharmonic Society had announced it would go on a year-round basis when it moved into its new home in Lincoln Center. It was thus becoming obvious that, if the Philadelphia Orchestra wanted to remain competitive in recruitment, it would have to move in this direction.

There were also pressures upon the Board from within the Philadelphia community. During the Orchestra strike of 1960, a Citizens' Committee to Save the Philadelphia Orchestra had been formed. This group, which was highly critical of the Board, had continued in existence for a time after the strike and had even attempted to solicit proxies to contest the incumbent Board members at the annual meeting. The Board was well aware that these individuals were prepared to resume their contest with the Association in the event of another strike.

Finally, the economic health of the Association was sufficiently good to enable it to make concessions at the time without undue sacrifice.[10]

As a result of all the above, a three-year contract was consummated in the autumn of 1963. It provided for an extension of the weeks of employment over the period of the contract, culminating in 52 weeks of salary with four weeks

of vacation for all Orchestra members in the third year
(1965–66 season). The weekly minimum salary was increased immediately from $190.00 to $200.00. Improvements
obtained in other conditions were: (1) a guarantee of one
day off each week (with the exception of four weeks in the
year); (2) a limitation of two services in one day; (3) 12
hours of free time after arrival from an out-of-town service;
(4) an average of four concerts per week during the symphonic season with only two five-concert weeks during that
period; (5) an oral commitment from the conductor to
limit Friday rehearsals to two hours whenever possible; (6)
the alteration of the non-renewal of contract procedure so
that a member of the Orchestra would have available to
him the substance of any charges prior to actual proceedings; (7) an increase in employer contributions to the
pension plan and a change in the voting procedures of the
committee which administered the plan so that the orchestra
members were given equality with the Association; (8) a
guarantee by the Association of full pension payments equal
to those due at age 65 to any Orchestra member with 25
years or more of service who might be dismissed for anything other than willful misconduct until such member
reached age 65 and could draw full pension benefits in the
normal manner.[11]

The prior contract of the 1962–63 season had provided
for 35 weeks of employment at a salary of $190.00 per week,
totaling $6,650.00. Earnings on an hourly basis for record-
ings totaled about $1,600. The Robin Hood Dell paid $165.00
per week for six weeks, or $990. Thus, the total minimum in-
come for the Orchestra and the Robin Hood Dell in the
1962–63 season was $9,245.00 for 41 weeks of work. The
new contract, in its third year, including a $2,000.00 guaran-
tee for recordings, totaled $12,400 for 48 weeks of work.

The new contract contained, in the third year, an exclusive services clause which required permission by the Association in order for any musician to perform with other musical groups of six or more. Conducting, teaching, or playing chamber music in groups of less than six was unaffected. The negotiating committee for the Orchestra members had calculated that the total income from such outside engagements which might be affected by this clause did not exceed $900.00. Moreover, a breakdown of the number of work hours expended in these engagements totaled slightly more than the work hours required in the additional seven weeks of employment under the new contract. Finally, whereas the outside work was performed during and in addition to full Orchestra weeks, the seven-week extension represented less work-hours spread over a longer period and was more in the spirit of the members' requests on working conditions, which sought relief from work load congestion.

The net result was an increase from about $10,140.00 to $12,400.00 annually over a three-year period without additional work for the majority of Orchestra members. These were the people who received the minimum wage and were therefore most likely to have performed the outside work. The new contract provided for the extension of all weekly salaries to 52, and thereby achieved an across-the-board principle which extended to the other Orchestra members whose salaries were above the minimum wage.

In the past, the Orchestra members had been represented in contract negotiations by the Executive Board of Local 77, American Federation of Musicians and an attorney, with the Orchestra members' committee present only as observers. The Association had been represented by two attorneys, the manager, and the assistant manager.

In the 1963 negotiations, at the request of the Association and after secret ballot approval by the Orchestra members, the union gave permission for three members of the Or-

chestra committee and two members of the pension committee to meet with five Board members of the Association
for an unspecified length of time. Periodic progress reports
were to be submitted to the union by the five Orchestra
members and the continuance of this type of negotiation
was to be at the discretion of the union.

The union saw fit to continue these meetings through the
summer of 1963, and they resulted in the above contract.
During this period there were also two full Orchestra membership meetings in which the salient features of the contract, as they were evolving, were explained.

At the conclusion of the negotiations, both committees,
feeling that this type of face-to-face subgroup meeting had
been fruitful, inserted a clause in the new contract providing
for the continuance of such meetings at the behest of either
committee to resolve any problems which might arise on a
day-to-day basis during the life of the contract.

The proposed contract was then reduced to writing by
attorneys for both sides and approved by both committees
at a final reading. It was then approved unanimously by the
Executive Board of Local 77 and submitted to a formal
ratification meeting of the Orchestra members in accordance
with the by-laws of the union. Three hours were spent in
reading and explanation and two hours in debate. The contract was then ratified in a secret ballot vote, 68 to 33.

The pact was extolled nationally as "a revolutionary new
approach to collective bargaining for symphony musicians"[12]
and for its unprecedented security of 52 weeks salary in the
symphonic field.[13] Secretary-Treasurer A. A. Tomei of Local
77 declared: "It's revolutionary. Symphony players simply
cannot exist from the income of a regular season."[14] Paul
Hume, Music Critic of the *Washington Post*, wrote of the
agreement: "a step which is absolutely necessary for any
orchestra which wishes to call itself first class. Musicians

who are forced to spend half the year, or nearly half, away from their music do not remain in top form."[15] The *Monthly Labor Review* of May, 1966, said: "The key negotiation for the 1963–64 season was the Philadelphia Orchestra's in which the first 52 week contract was reached."[16] In *The Culture Consumers*, Alvin Toffler, reporting an annual average earnings in 1961 of less than $4,000.00 from symphonic concerts for members of major symphony orchestras, declared: "When the Philadelphia Orchestra not long ago signed a contract guaranteeing its players 48 weeks of work per year plus a four-week vacation and minimum income of $12,400, it made musical history. This contract is a portent of the future."[17]

Nevertheless, within less than one year of the commencement of the contract and a year before the inauguration of its 52-week concept, the chairman of the Orchestra members' committee, who had chaired the negotiating committee, was defeated overwhelmingly for reelection[18] and a new chairman was selected who had been publicly opposed to the method of negotiation and the terms of the contract. Although labor relations previous to the 1963 contract had not been good, in the two years following the above change of leadership there were, in addition to a sizeable list of grievances submitted to the union, two arbitration proceedings (there had been only one in all previous labor relations), a federal court suit by the members of the Orchestra against the Association (there had been none in previous Orchestra history), and an eight-week strike (the longest in U.S. symphonic history up to that time).

The foregoing situation cannot be fully explained unless one is aware that there exists among the members of the Philadelphia Orchestra, in addition to an alienation from the management, an intense alienation from the work which they are called upon to perform.

ALIENATION FROM WORK

The following excerpt from an article which appeared in *Time* magazine is illustrative of the Philadelphia Orchestra situation in terms of work alienation. Entitled "Flying the Coop," it dealt with four outstanding string players of the Philadelphia Orchestra who had risked legal sanctions by resigning in less than the required notification period in order to become the resident string quartette at a university. The reason for their action was explained as follows:

> Nobody really sees him. Nobody really hears him. He is the fellow in the frayed white tie and tails, the one buried seven rows back peering sourly through a cluster of elbows. He is the symphony musician—bored, frustrated, and anonymous. So he didn't become the second Hiefetz as everybody in Glenn Falls said he would. There was nothing else to do but join a big-city symphony, file lock-step onto the stage—no talking please—and, at the nod of the imperious maestro, saw away mechanically at the Brahms "First" for the 101st time. . . .
>
> After all, no string player invests roughly twenty years and $25,000 for training to sit in the hundred-headed obscurity of a symphony orchestra. In his heart, if not in the ear of his audience, he is a full-fledged virtuoso who, says Los Angeles Symphony conductor Zubin Mehta, 'joins a symphony only as a last resort, and then is frustrated.' On the campus, however, he can assume the stature of a soloist, play largely what he wants—the way he wants to play it.[19]

The article then goes on to point to the increasing number of musicians who are leaving orchestras for college employment and quotes conductor Erich Leinsdorf, of the Boston Symphony, to the effect that the problem is essentially one of "loss of identity" in an orchestra, whereas the university offers an opportunity for more individual expression.

In a later article about the same quartette,[20] the members speak of the tremendous sacrifices which they made in order to play chamber music while members of the Philadelphia Orchestra, because the Orchestra itself afforded no such opportunity. Being in the Orchestra was "like a cog in a machine." One of the violinists says: "The difference between being a fiddler for the Philadelphia Orchestra and being a fiddler for the university is the difference between being an artist and being just a violinist among sixty other violinists." The duties at the university are described as being more varied and including—in addition to chamber music concerts—lecture discussions, coaching, and career guidance. Furthermore, they all expressed deep gratification at being able to select their own programs, interpret the music as they chose, and determine the time and length of their rehearsals.

George Rochberg, eminent American composer and former Chairman of the Music Department of the University of Pennsylvania, speaks as follows of what he describes as "the unhappiness and restlessness of orchestral musicians:"

> It is becoming increasingly clearer that orchestral musicians, especially the younger ones, want artistic freedom and mobility. They want music to be a vitalizing experience, not a daily grind which robs them of love for their art. Since they cannot find this in the musical organizations which make up the performance culture, they are—in increasing numbers—turning to the campuses of colleges and universities where they are freer to choose their own repertoire and to perform the new music of their contemporaries.[21]

During the long and bitter Philadelphia Orchestra strike of 1966, it was reported that a new factor had entered into symphonic labor relations. This was the "new breed of musician" who felt that he should have solo opportunities and had "an acute need to assert his individuality and ambitions by playing with smaller groups and by teaching.[22]

At this point it would be appropriate to present some examples from the literature of work alienation in order to offer a theoretical basis for this phenomenon.

The Hawthorne studies at the Western Electric Company[23] demonstrated that a work organization is really a social system within which people wish to be recognized and to satisfy psychological drives and social needs. In reporting this experiment, Mayo pointed out that the betterment of working conditions resulted in greater efficiency; but when, by prior agreement, the old conditions resumed, efficiency remained high. The content of the work itself had not changed, but its social aspect had. That is, individuals had been the object of attention and had been consulted about their wishes. In this way certain psychological needs for recognition had been fulfilled, even though the entire approach, from today's perspective, had strong implications of manipulation.

Out of work such as this came the Human Relations Movement, whose basic assumptions about work motivation threw new light on the problem of work alienation.[24] Traditional assumptions from economics held that people satisfied only an economic need at work, and that there existed an automatic mutuality of goals between individual and organization. The new assumptions, from the behavioral sciences, claimed that the individual sometimes behaves nonlogically (from an economic standpoint) in terms of rewards sought from work; that the social setting at work is frequently a behavior determinant; that the informal organization is a reality which affects and is affected by the formal organization; that there is no automatic perception of common goals between the individual and the organization; and that individual recognition is beneficial to morale.

A. H. Maslow[25] approaches the concept of work alienation by the construction of a hierarchy of human needs based upon the idea of prepotency or urgency of satisfaction. He postulates four such needs. These are Safety, Love, Esteem (the need for a high valuation of one's personal worth by oneself and others, the latter meaning recognition of achievement), and Self-Actualization (the need to utilize one's full potential and "to become everything that one is capable of becoming").

Erich Fromm, in *The Sane Society*,[26] views the full utilization of one's powers as a necessary precondition of mental health. He claims that, in the machine-like division of labor, the worker loses personal identification with the whole product such as the artisan or craftsman had before industrialization. The analogy here to many symphonic musicians is valid because, it will be demonstrated later, most of their training period is spent in the solo practice and performance of etudes, sonatas, and concertos wherein they experience personal identification with a product which is entirely theirs, whereas later, in the orchestra, their performance becomes an inaudible and unidentifiable component of a larger whole.

Another facet of alienation for Fromm is the situation where "he, the person, does not experience himself as the center of his world, as the creator of his own acts—where one is not related to oneself and the outside world productively."[27] Significantly, Fromm finds that, when creativeness and independent thought are balked, one "inevitable result" on the part of the worker is "destructiveness."[28] For Fromm, work is not only a necessity, it is what defines man as a social and independent being. He agrees with Marx that: "In the process of work, that is, the molding and changing of nature outside of oneself, man molds and changes himself."[29]

Fromm also maintains that work for individual economic rewards alone without engagement in the wider economic or social aspects of one's work is not a "meaningful human activity."[30] When the worker has no responsibility except the proper performance of his own task, when "he is put in a certain place, has to carry out a certain task, but does not participate in the organization or management of the work," the result is "a deep-seated, though often unconscious, hostility toward work and everything and everybody connected with it," because financial reward alone is an insufficient basis upon which to maintain self-respect.[31] Confirmation of this is found in a study by Walker and Guest in which auto workers manifested aversion to a job to the extent that it embodied repetition and mechanical characteristics.[32]

Fromm also addresses himself to the widely-held belief that man is naturally lazy. He maintains that laziness, "far from being normal, is a symptom of mental pathology."[33] That man, without the monetary incentive, would be driven by the boredom of inactivity to expend energy in a meaningful way. The best example is children, who, when they are healthy, are always busy. Fromm alludes to a body of available literature which demonstrates the adverse mental effects of inactivity upon unemployed workers and people forced to retire. He attributes the belief in natural laziness to the fact that alienated work is boring and unfulfilling, thus creating an aversion to it.

Wage incentive plans have been regarded by employers and union leaders as the answer to stimulation of effort and interest, but M. S. Viteles, using an Opinion Research Corporation survey,[34] shows that while a majority of workers (sixty-five percent vs twenty-two percent) regard incentive pay increases as more effective than hourly wages for increasing output, sixty-five percent vs twenty-nine percent favored the hourly wage over the incentive pay. Viteles interprets this as showing that although incentive pay may increase production, it does not solve the problem of obtaining the worker's cooperation, and in some cases may intensify that problem.

People may produce, then, and produce well (as in the case of the Philadelphia Orchestra), but this does not necessarily equate with self-fulfillment. A study by Goode and Fowler[35] demonstrates the coexistence of low morale and high productivity. In another study, Katz, Maccoby, and Morse[36] found no relationship between job satisfaction, satisfaction with the company, financial or status satisfaction, and productivity. Close supervision, although detrimental to morale, can increase production. There can be almost no closer type of work supervision than that exercised by the conductor of a symphony orchestra over the players. However, low productivity would be extremely difficult for the musician whose playing is a deep part of his ego structure (self-esteem). This therefore suggests that hostility engendered in the Philadelphia Orchestra job situation, which cannot be released in low productivity, may find its way into labor relations. Support for this idea can be found in a study by J. F. Lincoln[37] which traces an important link between lack of interest in one's work and industrial strife.

THE DISPARITY BETWEEN TRAINING AND JOB REQUIREMENT

The training of the Philadelphia Orchestra musician may be a contributing factor to his alienation from work. Expectations and skills are created in preparatory institutions which go beyond the narrow specialization required for the tradi-

tional repertoire and format to which he finds himself con-
fined. It has been shown that these expectations and skills
acquired in job preparation are important components of
self-fulfillment through work, and that when disparities exist
between the requirements of a job and the worker's training,
alienation can result.[38]

There are two types of musical institution from which
symphonic musicians are largely drawn. One is the music
conservatory, which specializes completely in training for
professional playing and grants the Diploma. The other is
the college, which grants the Bachelor of Music degree or
the Bachelor of Music Education.

Following are the minimum requirements of the typical
music conservatory for the Diploma on String, Woodwind,
or Brass instruments:[39]

(1) Three or more years of private instruction on the major
    instrument (confined to etudes, concertos, sonatas, scale
    studies, partitas, romances, and other selected compo-
    sitions for the instrument alone or with piano accom-
    paniment) are required.

(2) Solfege (sight singing): 1, 2.

(3) Dictation (notation of music by ear): 1, 2.

(4) Aural Harmony: 1.

(5) Elements of Music: 1.

(6) Piano: 1, 2 (for Strings), 1 (for Brass and Wood-
    winds).

(7) Chamber Music, Woodwind Ensemble, or Brass En-
    semble.

(8) Orchestra.

Following are the minimum requirements of the typical
music college for the Bachelor of Music degree, which is
described as "designed for those students who wish to prepare for full-time professional careers in performance:"[40]

(1) Private instruction on major instrument: 18 credit hours. (In the case of Violin, more than fifty compositions must be studied, all of which are for the instrument alone or with piano accompaniment.)

(2) Secondary Piano: 4 credit hours.

(3) Theory and Literature: 18 credit hours.

(4) Ear Training: 12 credit hours.

(5) English: 12 credit hours.

(6) General Studies Electives: 18 credit hours.

(7) Conducting: 4 credit hours.

(8) Orchestration: 2 credit hours.

(9) Music Elective: 8 credit hours.

(10) String Pedagogy: 2 credit hours.

(11) Music History: 6 credit hours.

(12) Ensemble Elective: 4 credit hours.

(13) Graduation Recital.

In the first example above, that of the music conservatory, it has been confirmed that the primary orientation is toward solo or chamber music playing.[41] The student is prepared and encouraged in this direction. Little attention is accorded to and little status is imputed to orchestral playing. Note that no orchestral repertoire is covered in the private instrumental instruction. There are no specified requirements for Orchestra. The Registrar explained that orchestra rehearsals take place sporadically and that attendance is desired but not enforced. A full schedule of solo and chamber music recitals is maintained but there is no scheduling nor does the school even possess facilities for public orchestral concerts.

In the second example above, that of the music college, much the same situation obtains. No orchestral music is covered in private instruction. It is possible, by electing each year an Ensemble other than Orchestra, to complete the four-year program without attending a single orchestra rehearsal. Many skills are acquired in such areas as Conducting, Orchestration, Pedagogy, and Music History which could never be utilized in the Philadelphia Orchestra job as it is currently constituted.

The logical goals and expectations of the musician who completes either of the above training programs could be expected to go beyond playing in a routinized and narrowly specialized symphony orchestra. This has been confirmed in interviews with professional musicians, music educators, and individuals involved in personnel work for symphony orchestras.[42] Given this situation, work alienation is a strong possibility.[43] Further confirmation of this is furnished by Dr. Bernard Borislow, Consulting Psychologist, who points out that the schools give the student a heavily self-centered, ego-building training which does not prepare him for subordination to a group or team. When he finds himself in the present orchestral situation, therefore, he may well experience unexpected frustration. Unsuccessful attempts to manipulate his environment can then lead to withdrawal or aggressive behavior.[44] As previously pointed out, one logical channel for such aggressive behavior is labor relations.[45]

In the case of the Philadelphia Orchestra, it is significant that of the 66 string players listed in the personnel for the 1966–67 season (the group which mounted the longest strike in U.S. symphonic history) 30 alone attended the music conservatory used as an example above.

ADDITIONAL STRESS FACTORS

There are additional stress factors inherent in the work procedures of the traditional symphonic format. One concerns the necessary method of rehearsal. Constant starting and stopping for corrections requires a large expenditure of energy on the part of the player to maintain his involvement because in such a large group the conductor is most often addressing another individual or section while the others must remain quiet and ready to resume playing instantly.

Performances, on the other hand, involve different physiological stress factors. Dr. Hugo Schmale, of the Max Planck Institute, has tested 1,397 musicians during performances with electrodes attached to the fingers, recorders to the ears, synthetic adrenalin and dionine injected under the skin, and wires under the clothing. Body temperature, heartbeat, and hypertension were read by instrument. Dr. Schmale concludes: "In no other profession are men subjected to as much collective time pressure and to as many stress factors as in an orchestra." He finds that nervous strain causes a decrease in blood circulation and lowers temperatures in the fingers. Illness, particularly cardiovascular and gastro-intestinal disorders, is high. Pulse beat increases from rehearsal to performance, air temperature rises about six degrees in the orchestra pit during the average opera performance, and tensions increase as the season progresses.

Dr. Schmale then goes on to furnish physiological evidence of how personal recognition for a musician can alter the stress factors of performance completely. Speaking of the legendary longevity of conductors, he says:

> There's a great difference between conductor and player. Conductors aren't subjected to the stress factors of collective discipline. They create the discipline—the promise of applause motivates a conductor to fight against the stress factors. But when does the average player ever feel that the accolades are meant for him personally? I have tested conductors and their pulse rates are phenomenal. But it's the prospect of exhilaration, not of stress.[46]

Another stress factor arises out of the relationship between the conductor and the musician.[47] McGregor has pointed out that no matter how we have resolved the emotional conflicts arising out of interdependent relationships in growing up:

> —we remain sensitive when we are placed in a situation which resembles, even remotely, the dependence of infancy. To be a subordinate in an organization is to be placed in a dependent relationship which has enough of the elements of the earlier one to be sensitive and, under certain conditions, explosive.[48]

The degree to which this "dependent relationship" is operative between the musician and the conductor has been described by Blackman.[49] He points out that the attention of the musician must be riveted upon the conductor, and declares: "each member of the orchestra relinquishes his individuality while subjecting his mind and body to the conductor—to allow every nerve and fiber of the body to receive and act on the conductor's communication."[50] The conductor, in turn, views his job from a standpoint of domination, where he must make of the men "a homogeneous sound—a tapestry."[51]

This all implies a degree of supervision which has few equals in other endeavors. Yet, this intimate working relationship between the conductor and the orchestra is, as the musician is sensitively aware, in sharp contrast to the great social and economic distinction which exists between them. Toffler points this out, and then goes on to add:

> When to this difference in standards of living the conductor adds pressure for discipline and a studied coolness toward the problems of his men, as some do, the steam generated can be explosive.[52]

Compounding this situation, audiences have placed the conductor on a pedestal as a symbol representing all those who are involved in the performance, to the understandable resentment of many fine orchestral players.[53]

Finally, the conductor, being a figure of great authority in such matters as dismissal, salary, and promotion, is not an inviting target for overt hostility. Often such felt hostility is more safely diverted against the impersonal edifice of management, with whom the conductor is identified by the orchestra.[54] Expressed another way, this is an example of Approach-Avoidance conflict where the individual must submit to what he perceives as the tyrannical authority of the boss or resign and face economic insecurity. By way of compromise, he accepts the role of pleasing the boss while at the same time he "retreats from the role of complete submission to retain some vestige of independence and self-esteem."[55] For some orchestral musicians, retention of self-esteem is accomplished by an uncompromising, militant attitude toward the management.

GOAL SUBSTITUTION

Part of the explanation for the seemingly contradictory conduct of the members of the Philadelphia Orchestra in demanding, achieving, and then reacting so negatively to year-round employment lies in the phenomenon of goal substitution. When the individual's goal of self-fulfillment is blocked in the organizational setting, it is not uncommon for him to substitute other goals as compensation.[56] This is not intended as any value judgment of the financial or work load demands which the Orchestra members have made, but is simply an explanation of one motivating factor among others which shapes the Orchestra musician's expectations of his job. The individual experiences dissonance (tension) when he perceives that he is expending effort and not reaching his goal. This dissonance can be reduced by finding something else in the situation to which value can be attached, in this case less work and more money as a form of personal recognition of artistic status.[57] Many a musician who is extremely concerned with rate of pay and work time limitations in the Orchestra will expend untold hours of individual practice or rehearsal for a solo recital or chamber music concert which brings him a comparatively small fee, if anything.

Therefore, while the 52-week contract did represent solutions for some of the musicians' economic needs, it did not accomplish changes which might have led to the satisfaction of those ego needs which are related to self-fulfillment on the job. On the contrary, for many members of the Philadelphia Orchestra the 52-week contract represented what is known in psychology as an Approach-Avoidance conflict.[58] The simultaneous attraction of year-round financial security bound to the extension of an alienated work situation (a goal with both positive and negative outcomes)[59] resulted in an ambivalent attitude for many Orchestra members.

By way of illustration, during the three years which followed the signing of the 1963 contract, there were many expressions of opinion among Orchestra members which amounted to a consensus about the undesirable length of a 52-week season and the error of having accepted it. Yet, when several opportunities presented themselves during this same period to discard the year-round concept, the members of the Orchestra showed no inclination to pursue them.[60] Instead, they continued to build their resentments until they exploded in the 1966 strike. This demonstrates that, when economic demands serve as substitutes for true self-fulfillment, the satisfaction of those demands only escalates the worker's dissatisfaction and leads to a new round of conflict.[61]

PART 2–LABOR RELATIONS IN THE PHILADELPHIA ORCHESTRA FROM 1963 TO 1966

THE RISE TO POWER OF THE MOST-ALIENATED

In its third year, the 1963 contract granted to the Association the privilege of undertaking new activities, one of which was Festival Weeks, to fill the additional period of guaranteed employment. Although inadvertently omitted in the language of the contract, all parties clearly understood that none of these new activities was permitted before the 1965–66 season. However, in November of 1963, three months after the signing of the contract, and without any previous consultation or preparation of the Orchestra members, the Association issued a press release announcing that the Orchestra, while on a transcontinental tour, would perform such Festival Weeks at the Long Island Festival of the Arts and at the National Music Camp in Interlochen, Michigan.

This created considerable consternation among the Orchestra members, and, judging by the large amount of time which the issue took up at subsequent meetings, it had a considerable effect upon the course of labor relations.

Although the Association quickly admitted its violation of contract and offered to rectify it by correctly classifying these services as Tour Weeks and compensating the Orchestra accordingly, disputes arose concerning tour bonuses and the reinsertion of an Association privilege of scheduling Sunday concerts on tour. This privilege had existed in the previous contract, had not been a subject of negotiation, and had simply been omitted by an oversight in the language of the new contract.

By September of 1964, although these services had already

taken place, no settlement of the various claims had been reached. In the meantime, a hard core group of Orchestra members, enjoying a strong consensus of opposition to the contract dating back to its negotiation and ratification, had become increasingly vocal. They maintained now that events justified their original contention that the contract was a bad one, and that it was now evident that the previous negotiations (face-to-face-subgroups of Orchestra members and Board) represented at best manipulation by the Board and at worst a sellout by the Orchestra members' committee. Moreover, they predicted even more dire consequences to come, such as the forced termination of the Robin Hood Dell, whose management had not enjoyed good relations with the Philadelphia Orchestra Board and which now had to contract for the Orchestra members' services through the Association.

Although the predictions of these people did not materialize, their arguments at the time undoubtedly influenced many Orchestra members. There existed, first of all, the continuing ambivalent attitude toward the 52-week contract which was pointed out previously. Second, there was a natural apprehension of the unknown, which in this case involved new and untried work situations ahead. Third, there was, as a result of years of bad labor relations, an uncertainty about the integrity of management and the prospects for any healthy working relationship with them.

It was at this time that new committee elections were held and the viewpoint of the hard core group gained ascendancy. The incumbent chairman was overwhelmingly defeated and a new committee was elected whose members were strongly identified with the opposition to the contract, and whose new chairman had also opposed the face-to-face subgroup type of negotiation.

The premises of alienation inherent in the Orchestra work

situation furnish adequate explanation for the rise of a hard core group of die-hards in opposition to a contract which represented to them the extension of their frustrations to a year-round basis. Such a sudden drastic change in a long-established pattern could be expected to produce changes in the interactive structure of the membership which would pose a challenge to the established leadership.[62] Furthermore, the Orchestra members' perception of their environment as threatening at this point, whether true or not, aided the hard core group to gain ascendancy. The concept of year-round employment which lay ahead undeniably involved a new way of life for all concerned, so that the immediate future was necessarily unpredictable. Such a situation gives rise to pressures to establish some kind of social reality, and its interpretation is vulnerable to emotion and the influence of subgroups.[63]

The new choice for committee chairman reflected the current attitude of the Orchestra membership. The individual chosen had not been able in the past to wield any significant influence in the group. Prior to his election, he had been a frequent but unsuccessful committee candidate, receiving only a small number of votes in each election. Most Orchestra members had considered his views as too radical and far out. Now, however, his militant stance suddenly attracted many votes.

The explanation of this lies in the Situational Approach to leadership. This holds that the situation or environment is the crucial variable in determining leadership, and not personal traits. Environmental change may well bring leadership change.[64] More specifically, group leadership may be viewed in terms of the attitudes and expectations of its members, how they perceive the external environment and who among the members will perform what they think should be done.[65]

In this case, discussions with Orchestra members revealed that most were convinced that they were in a threatening situation, were skeptical of management's intentions, and had, therefore, lost confidence in face-to-face communication as a method of problem-solving. One member summed up the attitude of many others when he explained his choice of the new chairman by saying: "Let's turn ____ loose on the Association and see what he can do."

From this point on (September, 1964), it will be shown that predominance in the decision-making of Orchestra membership business passed to this subgroup which had furnished the hard core opposition to the year-round contract. In order to more clearly delineate this group and trace its impact upon labor relations, it is useful at this point to establish specific criteria for identifying such persons, who shall be designated as most-alienated. These are the individuals who comprise the bottom strata of the Orchestra in terms of both self-fulfillment and economic rewards, and in whom, therefore, there is fused an alienation both from their work and from the management for whom they perform it. In order to be identified in this category, an Orchestra member fulfills both of the following qualifications: (1) receives no personal recognition performing solo or individual parts, but sits within a large string section beyond the first desk in which everyone plays identical parts; (2) receives the minimum or near minimum salary as set by the union contract, and thus always suffers relative deprivation. Given this degree of double frustration, hostility toward both the work and the organization can be shown to be a strong likelihood.[66]

One indication of the predominance of this group in Orchestra membership decision-making is the fact that the entire five-man committee which comprised the leadership of the Orchestra members after September, 1964 fell within this most-alienated category. Significantly, the predominance of most-alienated individuals in terms of participation at Orchestra membership meetings can also be demonstrated. A tabulation, taken from Orchestra membership minutes, of all speeches given, motions made and seconded, and questions raised and answered at Orchestra membership meetings covering a sample period from September 9, 1964 to February 26, 1965 shows that during this period there were 241 such floor actions. Of these, 187 were taken by most-alienated individuals. This group was comprised of only 27 persons. In effect, a most-alienated group which comprised twenty-five percent of the Orchestra took the lead in conducting seventy-seven and five-tenths percent (77.5%) of its business. Since the by-laws of the Orchestra members provide that 25 shall comprise a quorum and membership meetings rarely exceed 40, the picture emerges of a small determined group, bound by a common alienation, turning out for all meetings and guiding the destiny of all the Orchestra members. It is worth noting, as previously pointed out, that this same period was marked by a sharp escalation of labor conflict.

THE NEW METHOD OF LEADERSHIP AND SOME CONSEQUENCES

At the outset of the period which began in September of 1964, there was a crucial change in the method of exercising leadership of the Orchestra membership. The practice in the past had been for the Orchestra members' committee, after consultation with the union, the Orchestra members' attorney, or the management, to make recommendations to the body on the conduct of its business. However, in its first policy statement, the newly-elected committee declared that it would make no recommendations, but would instead allow the orchestra members to decide each issue "democratically" for themselves from the floor.

This laissez-faire type of leadership on the part of the new committee was understandable in view of the ostracism of the past Orchestra committee due to a belief among many Orchestra members that it had been taken in or had sold out. The new policy placed responsibility for all decisions upon the whole body and thereby protected the new Orchestra committee from possible recrimination by fellow Orchestra members. Under this type of leadership, however, the prognosis for effective and satisfactory problem-solving is very poor. It has been found most often to result in disorganization, failure, and setbacks. The former method of leadership, on the other hand, wherein elected leaders make recommendations for the approval of the body, is classified as democratic leadership, and has been found to be more effective for group functioning.[67]

Given the mutual distrust and suspicion which prevailed among the Orchestra members at this time, another predictable casualty, in addition to democratic leadership, was the continuing face-to-face subgroup meeting with the Board to resolve differences as they arose. The fear of membership criticism effectively deterred the Orchestra committee from maintaining any direct communication with the Directors.[68] There was one such meeting held on October 21, 1964 and none thereafter during this two-year period under study. Face-to-Face communication has been found to be the most effective method for preventing the escalation of labor conflict, and the abandonment of this procedure contributed to a hardening of attitudes which in turn drove the Orchestra committee even more rigorously to avoid contact with the Board out of fear of the reaction of its own constituents.[69]

Another factor inhibiting the effective conduct of business

by the Orchestra members was their apprehension or threat perception concerning the as-yet-untried aspects of the 52-week season. This had been intensified by the campaign of opposition to the new contract, accompanied by dire prophecies, which the most-alienated group had mounted in their successful bid for power. In such a situation, defensive behavior which reduces the ability to effectively deal with problems and choose correct or creative solutions was the predictable result.[70]

All the above factors—laissez-faire leadership, the isolation of the Orchestra members from any direct contact with their employers, and an atmosphere of intense threat perception— militated against the effective conduct of labor relations not only because of their own inherent defects, but also because they made the body at large more vulnerable to the domination of a vociferous group of most-alienated individuals.

To illustrate in a concrete way the effect of the above environment upon the conduct of labor relations by the members of the Orchestra, two important issues which were disposed of during the sample period have been selected for examination. The first issue had to do with the Long Island and Interlochen Festivals held in August and September of 1964. The Orchestra Board had originally acknowledged, at meetings with the prior Orchestra committee in December of 1963, that the prohibition of such festival weeks until the 1965–66 season had been intended by both sides and inadvertently left out of the wording of the new contract. Both agreed that these two weeks would therefore be treated as tour weeks under the contract in computing payment for extra services and Sunday premiums, with the exception that the management was not to pay a $10 weekly tour bonus since the Orchestra was in one place for each week and not actually traveling.[71] The management subsequently discovered that the privilege of scheduling

Sunday concerts during tour weeks, which had existed in the previous contract and which had not been in contention during the negotiations, had also been inadvertently omitted from the new contract. They asked that it be reinserted.

On October 16, 1964 the Orchestra members' attorney advised the new committee to recommend to the Orchestra members that they accept the financial settlement being offered and then taken a poll to determine their feelings on reinstating the management privilege of Sunday concerts on tour. [72]

However, at subsequent Orchestra membership meetings on October 23 and 24, in line with their new policy of laissez-faire, no recommendation was passed on to the membership by the Orchestra committee. Instead, those members present on October 26 voted, without secret ballot, to demand payment for extra services beyond those allowed in a tour week (something which had already been offered), the $10 weekly tour bonus, and denial of the Sunday tour concert.

The issue was then started through the grievance procedure as provided by the contract and came to arbitration before the American Arbitration Association on May 25, 1965. The arbitrator recommended that the Orchestra be paid for extra services beyond a tour week, and that they were not entitled to a $10 tour bonus. He also recommended that the issue of Sunday concerts on tour be brought to a vote of the Orchestra members, with the union and the Orchestra members' attorney agreeing to recommend to the members that they reinstate that privilege.

At this point in the arbitration, the Orchestra committee, in line with their policy, declared that they would not take the responsibility for accepting the arbitrator's recommendations and passing them on to the members of the Orchestra. The Orchestra members' attorney and the union officials present then declared that they would represent the Orchestra and accept the settlement on their own responsibility.

Later, on July 6, 1965, the attorney and union officials appeared before the entire Orchestra, stated that they considered the settlement fair, and recommended, therefore, that the Orchestra vote to reinstate the Sunday concert privilege. This time, with the full membership voting by secret ballot, the union position was in effect endorsed by an affirmative vote to reinstate the privilege.

In this case, an entire winter had been consumed in grievance procedures, charges and countercharges, and a costly arbitration to achieve results which had been available from the beginning and acceptable to a majority of the Orchestra members. When presented to them under conditions tending to reduce the effectiveness of the most-alienated group, namely, the furnishing of specific recommendations by persons in leadership (in this case, the attorney and the union), followed by a checkoff procedure enabling the entire Orchestra to vote by secret ballot, the members were able to act effectively.

The second issue centered on the Saratoga Festival at Saratoga, New York. In the contract negotiations of 1963 it had originally been intended to employ the Orchestra during August of the third or 52-week year at a summer festival. At that time, a citizens' committee of Pocono Mountain residents was in existence for the announced purpose of bringing the Philadelphia Orchestra to that area for a festival during the first three weeks of August, 1966. Success seemed likely inasmuch as the necessary land had already been secured. With this in mind, the negotiators envisioned a consecutive three-week vacation commencing the last week of August and extending to the end of the contract on September 14, 1966.

In the winter of 1963, however, the project, split by dissension and running into local opposition, fell through. The Philadelphia Orchestra Association, contractually obligated to provide employment during August of 1966, began to look elsewhere. In early 1964, an agreement was concluded for the Orchestra to be in residence at the Saratoga Performing Arts Festival in Saratoga, New York during August of 1966.

This caused consternation among the Orchestra members because the commitment at Saratoga ran three days longer than the projected Pocono Festival and thereby violated the contract, inasmuch as the ensuing three-week vacation extended the contract three days beyond its expiration to September 17.

In early 1964, after the announcement of the Saratoga Festival, a meeting was held between the old committee (they were not displaced until September of 1964) and the Board of Directors. The Directors offered to pay for the additional days at Saratoga as extra services, to then provide a 21-day vacation immediately following Saratoga, to pay for the week of September 18, which began the new contract year on a Wednesday, as a full week back to the preceeding Monday, and to provide an extra week of vacation during the preceding spring as additional compensation.[73]

This offer was reported to the membership, but no action was taken before the change of leadership in September of 1964. After that, with the prevailing atmosphere of distrust and suspicion, the method of laissez-faire leadership, and the discontinuance of communication with the Board, the Orchestra members became impotent to resolve the issue. The chronicle of membership meetings from October 21, 1964 to August of 1966 (after the Festival had been performed) on this subject is a record of bickering, delay, uncertainty, confusion, and distrust.[74] Even the urging of the union could not bring the Orchestra members to agree to negotiate, let alone agree upon the terms for which they would settle.[75] At one point, the members of the Orchestra passed a by-law which in effect forbade their representatives from meeting with the management even to discuss the issue.[76] The record reveals that they could not agree upon whether to negotiate, who would represent them if they did negotiate, and what their conditions for settlement would be.

Finally, in August of 1966, the union, seeing that the Orchestra members were paralyzed and incapable of acting, stepped in and made a settlement with Association attorneys. The Orchestra members realized considerably less than even the Association's original offer. They were paid for extra services, as originally offered, but gained no extra week of vacation or full week's salary for a half week's work at the start of the following season, which had been part of management's original offer. In fact, since the season ended on September 18, the union allowed the new season to begin on September 23, and the Orchestra members lost five days of salary.

The bitterness growing out of this issue further inflamed the members of the Orchestra toward the management, and, coming as it did, just before the opening of negotiations for the new contract, contributed in no small measure to the long and bitter strike which ensued.

The disposition of the above issue is symptomatic of the malaise which prevailed in the labor relations of the Philadelphia Orchestra during this sample period.[77] Ineffective problem-solving increased the frustrations of the Orchestra members, which in turn resulted in increased hostility toward the management. Management reacted with increased hostility toward the members of the Orchestra and became convinced that no negotiations with them or peaceful solutions to problems were possible.[78] There was a steady deterioration of labor relations over the two-year period; so that, by the time negotiations were scheduled to begin for a new contract in 1966, the hardening of attitudes and accumulated hostility on both sides precluded anything but a bitter strike. Although direct causal relationships are difficult to establish for every specific situation, there can be no doubt that the deep and bitter alienation from both the organization and the work which prevails among Philadelphia Orchestra members was in no small part responsible for this state of affairs.

Labor Strife and the Future of the Organization

The Philadelphia Orchestra Association has followed policies which have earned it the distinction of being the most economically and efficiently run major symphony in the United States.[79] These accomplishments, however, have taken place, for the most part, at the expense of the musicians of the Orchestra, either through economic deprivation or personal frustration due to the extreme routinization necessary to efficient operation. It is hardly surprising, therefore, that the Philadelphia Orchestra Association has also earned the more dubious distinction of having the poorest labor relations of any major symphony in the United States.[80] It has had more strikes and public disputes of longer duration than any similar organization.[81] While it is not possible to minutely analyze this whole record in terms of causal relationship, the above analysis of the causes and effects of alienation strongly suggests that it is a crucial and continuing problem in labor relations.[82]

The state of its labor relations may, in turn, be crucial to the survival of the Philadelphia Orchestra. There is evidence that the bitter labor strife which characterized the 1966 strike has particularly dysfunctional aspects for a non-profit organization that is dependent upon public support. During this strike, the Association and the Orchestra members engaged in acrimonious public exchanges. The Association made statements which implied that the musicians were already quite well paid for comparatively little work. The musicians, in turn, charged the Association with falsely pleading poverty while concealing large assets, and made various other charges calculated to weaken public confidence in the leadership of the organization.[83]

One result of this was that, after the strike ended, the Association encountered resistance among some past contributors who, influenced by the statements made by the Association during the strike, now believed that the musicians were unduly affluent and over-compensated for the amount of work that they performed. On the other hand, the professional survey commissioned by the Association after the strike in preparation for the Philadelphia Orchestra Challenge Program discovered that potential contributors expressed reluctance to support an organization which they now thought might actually be concealing unused resources. In addition, members of the business community expressed a lack of confidence in a management which permitted such a deterioration of labor relations, and held reservations about committing support to an organization whose survival might be jeopardized by the intensity of its internecine warfare.[84] The survey emphasized in no uncertain terms that, if the Association was to generate the magnitude of public support necessary to survival in an era of rapidly rising costs of operation, it must improve its public image, and that one crucial area in this respect was labor relations.[85]

Thus, in summation, labor alienation in the Philadelphia Orchestra can be viewed within a cause and effect progression; bureaucratization leading to alienation, leading to labor conflict, leading to loss of public confidence and support. If the organization does eventually perish because of an inability to resolve its internal conflicts, it may be due in no small measure to its overriding dedication to economy and efficiency.[86] Therein may lie a valuable lesson for organizational theory as related to non-profit institutions which are dependent upon public contribution. It may become necessary to add a new dimension to the definition of what constitutes rational organizational behavior. Indeed, it may be possible that economy and efficiency of operation, which Weber postulated as attributes contributing to the superiority of modern bureaucracy over preceding forms, can be rather viewed along a functional-dysfunctional continuum where at some point a human behavior feedback is generated sufficient to cause organizational destruction. In this sense what may then appear on the surface to be rational organizational behavior could, in the longer run, prove to be pathological.

It must be remembered, however, that in the case of an organization such as the Philadelphia Orchestra, the making of policy adjustments is not a simple matter. For one thing, the value structure of the leadership, who are mostly businessmen, puts a high premium on economy and efficiency. For another thing, this institution is a non-profit organization forced to rely upon its own resources in a private market economy, which severely restricts its leeway to act. It may well be that this problem can only be resolved by some form of external intervention. This will be explored further at the conclusion of this study.

Chapter V

Some Additional Costs of Bureaucratization

FAILURE TO SERVE CONTEMPORARY MUSIC AND THE CULTURAL NEEDS OF THE COMMUNITY

Individuals eminent in the musical field agree that, at the present time, most composers are not writing for the symphony orchestra.[1] The reasons usually advanced as an explanation for this are the difficulty of securing a performance in the face of tight scheduling (new works require more time for preparation than familiar old ones) and box office considerations.[2] The modern symphonic organization, in its pursuit of efficiency and economy, expends very little for the commissioning of new works. Yet, composers are faced with the prospect of making a living, to say nothing of the prohibitive cost of producing a master score and instrumental parts for a full symphony orchestra.[3] Even where symphonic organizations offer commissions to prominent composers, the latter are reluctant to accept because they know that all too often their work will not become part of the orchestra's repertoire on a continuing basis, but will be utilized as a vehicle for publicity in a premiere and a few subsequent performances, and never played again.

Another explanation advanced for the lack of new music

for symphony orchestras is that many contemporary composers feel restricted within the traditional symphonic format, as exemplified by the use of the entire orchestra (full strings, brass and woodwind choirs, and percussion).[4] This viewpoint holds that a new kind of music was ushered in by such composers as Schoenberg and Stravinsky, which is best expressed in small and unusual groupings of instruments.[5] Symphonic organizations, however, suffering from bureaucratic hardening of the arteries, are reluctant to make innovations in their traditional routine.[6]

The result, according to Leonard Bernstein, perhaps the best known figure in American music today, is that the symphony orchestra has become a museum, simply a repository of the past.[7]

George Rochberg, eminent American composer and former Chairman of the University of Pennsylvania Music Department, has defined this growing estrangement of symphonic and operatic organizations from new music and formats as a divorce of the "performance culture" from the "creative culture."[8] He declares:

> I am not the first to call the opera houses and concert halls museums and, if things continue the way they are, I will not be the last. Their repertoires are essentially static, *fait accompli,* and the habits of performance and response they engender are, by now, almost totally lacking in relevance to contemporary experience and the new possibilities of music.
>
> I remember one of the curators of the performance culture saying to me many years ago that 'the Philadelphia Orchestra is no place for experiments.' As a member of the Board of that orchestra, he was defending the values of the Establishment by sacrificing the present to the past.
>
> Those involved in the creative culture of today are seeking ways and means of making music—its composition and its

performance—entirely different from the past. An occasional rapprochement with the performance culture does not alter the direction now being taken by the creative culture. . . . A generation ago it was still the ambition of young composers in America to write for the orchestra; but today they rarely write orchestral music unless they are asked to—and such invitations are few and far between. . . . Because conductors, orchestra boards, managers, impresarios, etc., are the curators of the musical establishment and believe only in what *has been* successful, the repertoire is virtually sealed off from the present.[9]

Symphonic organizations, the Philadelphia Orchestra included, have failed to serve the art of music so far as they have failed to provide encouragement and exposure for those who are currently creating music and setting its new directions.

The failure does not end here, however. The refusal to provide a forum for the new music is not only a disservice to the art of music, it is also an abandonment of responsibility for the cultural awareness and education of the community. Rochberg declares:

It is shocking to realize that between the performance culture, which still dominates the musical life of our society, and the creative culture, which is still trying to alter and extend the range of musical consciousness, there is virtually no real communication.[10]

The result is that the appreciation and understanding of symphonic audiences for the most part ends with Tchaikovsky, Brahms, and Beethoven. This is directly attributable to the programming policies of organizations like the Philadelphia Orchestra whose cultural hegemony makes them the arbiters of community cultural standards. They have made themselves the staunch champions of the past because it has been economically profitable for them to do so, and because it suits the conservative tastes of the upper class. For the same reasons, they have set their faces firmly against the present and the future.

IMPLICATIONS FOR ORGANIZATIONAL SURVIVAL

The long-range implications of this failure to serve contemporary music and community cultural needs cannot be subjected to much empirical investigation at the present time. Only speculation and a certain amount of as-yet-inconclusive evidence about trends in audience attendance at symphonic concerts are available. The speculation herein presented, however, is by musical notables with impressive credentials and, therefore, should be accorded some weight.

Elliott Carter, one of the most eminent American composers, declares:

> I think that unless the situation changes very drastically, not only will there be no future for new music in the symphony world, but the symphony world itself will die; because it seems to me that a museum exists in the context of other museums. The old art is only interesting as it seems living to us, and it seems living to us because we are surrounded also with contemporary art. Once an art is a completely distant and dead thing, it is no longer even worth conserving, except as a kind of curio.
>
> Now we've come to the point where Beethoven requires new halls because in the old halls people are beginning to be bored even with the performers, so they have had to put halls in new locations and fill them with air-conditioning so that Beethoven is still tolerable—instead of looking for some new music to play. This seems to me very unfortunate, and if this is not changed, finally even the buildings will not be enough to hold interest in the music profession. Therefore, I maintain that it is headed for disaster, at least as we know

it, unless the symphony orchestra takes a very rapid series of strides to bring the audience more interest in contemporary music.[11]

Lukas Foss, well-known composer and conductor of the Buffalo Philharmonic, views the problem in a similar manner:

> So maybe it is true that the symphonic dream is no longer alive—certainly not the typical symphony orchestra composed of woodwinds in twos and threes, brasses in twos and threes, four horns, strings, percussion. That typical idea . . . is no longer exploitable. But more than that, with Beethoven there came into the symphony that which we really call the symphonic, which is basically a heroic expression, and the symphony orchestra—particularly as embodied by the old-fashioned conductor—somehow underlines this heroic concept of the finale building up toward victory. This heroic expression no longer rings true. So unless we can rescue the symphony orchestra from that particular expression, it is finished.[12]

George Rochberg agrees, and sees the loss of future audiences as a result:

> The official performance culture itself stands in danger of destroying the very forms it seeks to preserve. The orchestra, as we know it, began around 1840, the opera around 1600. Both are social institutions in addition to fulfilling artistic functions, and, as social institutions, are as much subject to the forces of growth and decay as any other institution. Neither is sacrosanct. If they insist on living in the past, it is a certainty they will not live into the future in any real sense; for to get there, they must use the present as a bridge and it is precisely their refusal to acknowledge the present which endangers their continuation. It is not likely that the younger generations, thoroughly disaffected

with the values of the world they are growing up in, are going to support a culture whose relevance to *their* world is practically nonexistent. Sensitive young people today respond more readily to Stravinsky, Schoenberg, jazz, and the Beatles than they can to Beethoven or Wagner. If the repertoire is dead to the present and if those who live in that present demand relevant and vital experience of the culture around them, then it is possible to predict the eventual demise of the forms of that culture, in the case of music specifically, the orchestra and the opera.[13]

At the present time it is not possible to assess the validity of the above predictions. There are, however, some scattered intimations that attendance at symphony orchestra concerts may already be declining. *The New York Times* reports that concert attendance in that city is variously estimated to have currently declined from seven to forty percent.[14] At the New York Philharmonic's Great Performers series, there was only one completely sold house during the 1968 concert season. Established artists, whose names are ordinarily guarantees of sold out auditoriums, have been drawing partial houses.[15] Even more serious, people in the concert management field are agreed that the loss is principally among the younger audiences, who are gravitating to rock concerts and art films. One reason cited for this is a failure to exploit new ideas in concerts. One prominent manager declares: "It's the same old tired people doing things in the same old tired way."[16]

A decline in subscriptions to the Boston Symphony Orchestra (where they were once "Like Standard Oil of New Jersey, like U.S. citizenship itself—to keep and bequeath, not to sell and buy") has recently been reported.[17]

The manager of the Philadelphia Orchestra was evidently reflecting a concern about future audiences when he publicly questioned whether his organization was doing enough to attract new young audiences in Philadelphia.[18]

Finally, when the Philadelphia Orchestra recently made a change in its long-established subscription format, the results, according to one staff member, were unexpectedly disconcerting. The Friday–Saturday subscription series had for many years been based upon a 28-week winter season. These subscriptions had, for the most part, been sold on a 14- or 28-week basis. The 1968–69 winter season, however, was extended to 30 weeks at the same time that the 28-week subscription was reduced to 24 weeks. This enabled the Association to offer a new series of six Friday and Saturday evenings in the hope of attracting new subscribers. To the consternation of the Association, however, large numbers of 14- and 28-week subscribers promptly applied for the new series, indicating that they wished to drop their longer subscriptions. This implication of slackening audience interest, according to the staff member, was not lost upon the Association.

At the present time there exists another long-term threat to the survival of institutions such as the Philadelphia Orchestra which arises out of the inflationary nature of the economy. Baumol and Bowen, in a recent study entitled *Performing Arts: The Economic Dilemma*,[19] have brought out a major problem which will increasingly plague performing arts organizations—that in an era of steadily mounting costs they are unable to compensate by increasing their productivity due to the nature of their product and its unchanging method of hand production. The prognosis is for a steadily widening gap between income and costs of operation. Moreover, the authors dispel the myth of a cultural explosion in the United States since World War II in terms of audience growth and character. They estimate that in 1963–64 the audience attending the live performing arts totaled no more than two and one-half to three million people, or slightly more than two percent of all United States residents 18 years or older.[20] This would indicate that the audience growth relative to total population has not been significant. Furthermore, this audience is shown to be well-educated, of high income, and drawn mainly from the professions. It is, therefore, hardly representative of the general population. This audience profile furnishes confirmation for something which has already been brought out in this study —that the Philadelphia Orchestra seeks, for economic reasons and because of the class bias of its leadership, to serve only the select elites of the community who can afford its services.

Predictably enough, in view of the audience profile above, the bulk of private support for these organizations comes from individuals in the upper income groups. The indications are, however, that they have chosen a slender reed upon which to lean. Baumol and Bowen show that the proportion of the nation's wealth and income flowing to these upper income groups has been steadily declining, and their contributions as a group to philanthropies have not increased as much as those of other individuals since 1954.[21] Therefore, the prognosis for increased giving from this source is not good. One of the top officials of the Philadelphia Orchestra Association has declared publicly that large symphony orchestras are doomed because their particular sources of private support cannot keep up with mushrooming costs.[22]

Other areas of support which the authors examine offer little reason for encouragement. Foundations, for example, are oriented toward providing seed money; that is, funds calculated to furnish impetus toward some goal. These grants are most often "one-shot" and not renewable, being intended to stimulate other sources of support. Yet, if Baumol and Bowen are correct, as performing arts organizations become more mature and established, their gap between income and costs of operation can be expected to grow even more rapidly. Thus, the foundation does not offer the type of sustained support which these organizations will need in order to survive.[23]

Corporate support of the arts has been shown to be negligible.[24] Moreover, increased giving from this source will in all likelihood be directed toward the explosive social, economic, and physical problems of the urban environment.

An examination by Baumol and Bowen of government support of the arts indicates that it has been extremely small. Municipalities have the best record in this respect. However, in view of their present financial plight and their lack of fiscal independence under our federated governmental structure, it is unlikely that much more support can be expected from this source.

There is evidence at the present time that the Baumol and Bowen prognosis may already be coming true. In a recent report, the Ford Foundation finds that the arts are facing a grim financial picture in America, and notes that several major artistic organizations are in danger of financial collapse.[25] One of the principal reasons advanced is that inflationary costs are overrunning income.

It has been suggested that the answer lies in creating a larger audience by increased exposure of the arts.[26] This solution (bringing the arts to more people) is a proper social goal, but it begs the economic issue. The whole point of the Baumol and Bowen thesis in this respect is that every time a performing arts organization does its "thing" it loses money. Deficit, even with full attendance, is an inherent part of the process; and increased activity, particularly for lower-paying audiences, will only bring increased deficit. The economic dilemma of organizations like the Philadelphia Orchestra can be summed up as follows: they are forced to exist by their own resources under a private economy which dictates that they follow policies of bureaucratic rationality; this, plus the class bias of the leadership as in the case of the Philadelphia Orchestra, leads them to serve a small elite audience from whom they derive the greatest profit; this elite, being the recipient of their services, has become the source of their support through contributions; but the inflationary trend of operational costs now threatens to outdistance the ability or willingness of this group to continue its support.[27]

In view of all the above, there is a real possibility that the symphony orchestra, as we know it, may cease to exist. This does not mean, however, that it cannot be transformed so that it becomes a vital institution for serving the needs of the community and the art of music.

This transformation is worth the attempt. For one thing, the symphony orchestra bridges the gap between the American public and serious music. For this reason, it has a great potential for educating and elevating the musical consciousness of America. As the arbiter of community cultural standards, its influence is enormous, and the presentation of new music under its auspices would be a potent factor making for public acceptance. It also possesses institutional know-how and resources which could be put to work for more beneficial purposes. Some of these are: the accumulated experience of putting on concerts on an almost daily basis year after year; a large pool of top-notch talent; physical facilities and equipment; and institutional bulwarks such as endowment funds, regular contributors, and organized volunteers.

There is also the consideration of what the fate of the new music will be if its promulgation is left to a scattering of tiny esoteric musical societies, sporadic performances in inferior facilities, and a few progressive college campuses (where, in most cases, it leads a tentative existence because it has a low budgetary priority). The symphony orchestra has the potentiality for establishing a bridge between the creative culture and a sizable audience. Without this, the new music stands in danger of becoming a small movement existing marginally upon the periphery of American culture, whose adherents speak only to themselves.

Finally, the question is still open for debate as to whether we are ready, by allowing the symphony to die, to relegate the masterworks of the past to oblivion, so that they are no longer played at all. If Michelangelo and Leonardo can still speak to us, why cannot Bach and Beethoven continue to be played in moderation? Gustav Mahler, for example, is hardly contemporary, yet the timelessness of his music apparently holds great attraction for many young people today.[28]

All in all, in spite of its present serious deficiencies, the symphony orchestra is worth transforming. If one accepts this premise, the next crucial question is, how can it be made into a more socially and culturally responsive institution?

Conclusion

In 1936 the prognosis for the Philadelphia Orchestra was hardly encouraging. It had sustained the loss of both the charismatic leader who had sparked its rise and the large individual donors who had furnished its economic base. Moreover, the country was in the throes of a severe depression that was causing a decline in general contributions and concert attendance.

Yet today, we find this organization still existing and appearing, on the surface, to be relatively secure. Inasmuch as our private economy forces such institutions to depend entirely upon their own resourcefulness, the very survival of the Philadelphia Orchestra in itself represents an administrative accomplishment.

The key to this accomplishment, in addition to maintaining professional excellence, has been bureaucratization, meaning that all policies and operating procedures have been rationalized to strictly conform to overriding goals of economy and efficiency; and, once developed, these procedures have been routinized on a day-to-day and year-to-year basis with no significant deviation. In some respects the present position of the Philadelphia Orchestra supports Max Weber's contention as to the superiority of the bureaucratic over all preceding forms of organization.

However, upon closer examination, this facade of accomplishment and organizational strength reveals serious deficiencies which spell grave trouble over the long run for the

Philadelphia Orchestra. This has come about because the same bureaucratic policies which have up to now enabled it to survive have at the same time been exacting a heavy cost in artistic, social, and individual terms which are unaccounted for in Weber's theory. These costs now pose a real threat to the future existence of the organization.

One such cost is a deep alienation on the part of some members of the Orchestra from both the work which they perform and the management of the organization in which they perform it. The former is due to the repetitive and routinized nature of a bureaucratized work situation which makes no allowance for self-fulfillment or individual recognition, and the latter arises out of a long history of exploitation due to bureaucratic policies of stringent economy. This alienation has shown itself capable of generating and escalating labor conflict to a point where public confidence and financial support have been seriously jeopardized. At the present time this alienation continues unabated and is a catalyst for the resumption of internal conflict that could ultimately tear the organization apart.

Another cost has been a lack of service to the community. The Philadelphia Orchestra plays for only small select elites in Philadelphia and other areas. The less advantaged and the young people of its own community have been ignored.

It is hardly surprising, therefore, that the vital economic support of the Orchestra from contributions comes principally from this same small upper class whose cultural needs it serves. At the present time, however, the proportionate contributions to philanthropy of this group relative to other segments of the population is declining; and, as the operating expenses of organizations like the Philadelphia Orchestra continue to mount in an inflationary economy, there is a very real possibility that they will outdistance the ability or the willingness of this small group to continue its support. A

Ford Foundation study has found that this may already be happening. Moreover, corporate, foundation, or municipal support, as Baumol and Bowen have shown, is not likely to be available to close the gap.

The Philadelphia Orchestra has also neglected its responsibility for raising community cultural standards. In pursuing programming policies designed to maximize revenue from ticket and record sales, it has served its audiences the same conservative fare and formats year after year. As a result, Philadelphia audiences are known for their conservatism. Their musical awareness is severely limited, and there is a large body of new and unfamiliar music and formats of which they have little or no understanding.

The Orchestra has also allowed economic considerations to take precedence over its responsibility to advance the art of music. The same deference to the box office which has necessitated conservative programming and unchanging formats has also ruled out the presentation of a fair representation of contemporary music. In addition, the tight schedule of the Orchestra allows only rare performances of such music because more time is required for preparation. This time cannot be spared because the greatest revenue can only be obtained by playing as many concerts as possible with a minimum of time expended for rehearsal.

One outcome of this situation has been pictured as a divorce of the performance culture from the creative culture. Composers are not writing for the symphony orchestra. In the opinion of some eminent musicians, the orchestra is in danger of becoming a museum which is simply a repository of the past, having little or no relevance to present day culture or audiences, especially the young people. At the present time there are scattered intimations that it may already be suffering a decline in attendance. If this continues as a trend, the symphony orchestra will face extinction.

The Philadelphia Orchestra now faces a basic dilemma. It is currently following bureaucratic policies of economy and efficiency whose costs threaten to destroy it. Yet, it is driven to follow these policies by two basic considerations: (1) it is a non-profit organization forced by a private market economy to depend upon its own resourcefulness for survival; and (2) these same policies serve to perpetuate a small upper-class elite in the leadership of the Orchestra, from which position they derive prestige and social recognition and utilize the organization to serve the cultural and social needs of their own class. Moreover, since they are primarily businessmen, goals of economy and efficiency are very congenial to their own personal value structures and therefore continue to enjoy a high organizational priority.

A solution must be found which will both guarantee the survival of the Philadelphia Orchestra and at the same time justify that survival by making it into an institution which will better serve both the total community and the art of music. The first step of such a solution would be the provision of substantial federal and/or state subsidy. Given the demonstrated inadequacy of private, corporate, foundation, or municipal support, this remains the only viable alternative that can break the economic straightjacket of the private market economy and the stranglehold of the upper class to provide the necessary flexibility and leeway for the organization to change its operational policies.

Some activities which could be underwritten by public funds are: low cost and free concerts for wide segments of the community, including students, youth, and ghetto residents; the commission and performance of new works for symphony orchestra; performances in smaller cities and towns of the state which cannot at present afford the Orchestra as a concert attraction; mixed media concerts using other art forms in conjunction with music; concerts for working people in industrial or labor union facilities; concerts for the elderly; and concerts in suburban areas in the larger shopping centers. In addition, it would become possible to set aside a short period during the year when the Orchestra would read new works and give composers a chance to hear what they have set to paper. This same period could be used to give talented young orchestra players a chance to gain the experience of playing alongside seasoned professionals, and aspiring conductors a chance to observe rehearsal techniques and have the opportunity of working with a professional organization. Subsidy would also make possible the presentation of many new young soloists who normally experience great difficulty in securing public appearances because they have not as yet become box office attractions.

The Orchestra could be subdivided into small units which would make possible a wide variety of additional activities. There could be chamber music and concerts performing the new music for small groups. Concerto ensembles featuring members of the Orchestra in solo roles would also be possible. Members of the Orchestra could conduct seminars for music students at educational institutions. Small groups would have the flexibility to give concerts in the public schools and meet personally with aspiring students for career guidance. Some members of the Orchestra could work within community programs such as Headstart. Others could make a contribution in music therapy at local institutions. Once the economic and class constrictions are relaxed by the provision of public funds, there would probably be a flood of creative proposals for community and artistic service from a variety of quarters, including the Orchestra members themselves.

The above proposals offer a reasonable hope of alleviating the more serious threats to the Philadelphia Orchestra. For one thing, subsidy will provide a reasonable base of support for the inflationary period ahead. For another thing, the commissioning of new works and the performance of more contemporary music, both in the large orchestra and in the smaller group format, should establish a new close relationship between the creative and the performance cultures which will insure that the symphony orchestra remains a vital and relevant institution to present and future audiences. Finally, small group and individual activities will present Orchestra members with the opportunities for self-fulfillment and recognition which are so badly needed to alleviate the intense professional alienation that currently exists. The chances for organizational survival will be greatly enhanced and the Philadelphia Orchestra will become an institution which truly serves the whole community and the art of music.

Public subsidy alone, however, is only the first step to attaining the above objectives. Even if the monies were available, it is doubtful whether the organization possesses the administrative know-how to make contact with and move into all these new areas.

The second step to a solution, therefore, must be the creation of a new professional, the arts administrator, who will plan and direct the above programs. At the present time, many arts organizations, finding themselves in great difficulty, have asked the universities to institute the training of such professionals. Research is currently being conducted in a curriculum at Drexel University. Most art organizations, however, do not think in terms of public subsidy and, therefore, envision the arts administrator as some sort of super salesman who will be able to come up with new and slicker ways to package and merchandise their product, extract money from donors, and wring even more economy out of organizational operations. If this study has demonstrated anything, however, it has shown that this course has definite limitations. Most of the present threats to the survival of arts organizations are the direct results of such policies.

The need is for a curriculum that will broadly define the role of an arts administrator, and that will produce individuals who can furnish creative leadership in charting the future course of arts programs in this country. Such persons must understand the broad forces that are currently moving American society toward profound changes. They must grasp both the promise and the threat of modern technology and organization, and seek to nurture the creative forces in man. Above all, they must grasp the imagery, communication, and response that art is capable of evoking, and put it in the service of modern man to help him define himself in a world changing with awesome speed.

Finally, the arts administrator will only be able to perform his job properly if he is answerable to a democratic Philadelphia Orchestra Board of Directors which represents a wide social and economic spectrum of the community. Members of the Orchestra, other professional practicing musicians, the black communitiy, city government, organized labor, and educators are some of the elements that should be represented upon the Board. Given the class bias and the limited concept of community and artistic service of the present leadership, it is not reasonable to assume that they would agree to follow the above programs even if the funds were forthcoming. Because it is difficult to justify the expenditure of public monies to support all such organizations which serve only to the cultural needs of an affluent minority, some stipulations or guidelines may be attached to government grants. However, given the heavy representation of *Social Register*, wealth, and business and industrial leaders on the boards of directors of leading cultural organizations, it is unrealistic to assume that government agencies could affect really significant changes in policy over the opposition of such a powerful clientele. In the case of all such elitist cultural organizations, only a truly representative board of directors which speaks for all sections of the community can furnish the impetus and direction from within to cooperate with arts administrators and government agencies in moving the institution in the right directions.

If the three steps suggested above—substantial public subsidy, a new type of arts administrator, and a representative board of directors—can be brought about, then institutions like the Philadelphia Orchestra will be able to make magnificent contributions to their communities and to American culture. Let us hope that the reality is not too far into the future.

Notes

Chapter I

[1]John H. Meuller, *The American Symphony Orchestra* (Bloomington: Indiana University Press, 1951), pp. 25–29.

[2]Ibid., p. 124.

[3]Ibid.

[4]Frances Anne Wister, *Twenty-Five Years of the Philadelphia Orchestra* (Philadelphia: Philadelphia Women's Committees for the Philadelphia Orchestra, 1925), p. 13.

[5]Ibid., p. 13, p. 19.

[6]Ibid., p. 14. Also Meuller, p. 125. Describes the conflict between the Theodore Thomas and Walter Damrosch factions. When Thomas was not selected for the inaugural concerts, his patron boycotted the new project. A move to raise $100,000 to bring Damrosch and his New York Symphony Society to Philadelphia met violent opposition and was dropped.

[7]Wister, p. 19.

[8]Ibid., pp. 33–34, 38–39, and 41.

[9]Meuller, pp. 125–126.

[10]Ibid., p. 126.

[11]Wister, p. 101.

[12]Philadelphia Orchestra Association, *Fiftieth Anniversary Season* (Philadelphia: By the Author, 1950), p. 8. Cites the *Public Ledger,* October 12, 1912.

[13]Wister, p. 100.

[14]Meuller, p. 128.

[15]H. H. Gerth and C. Wright Mills, *From Max Weber: Essays*

in Sociology (New York: Oxford University Press, 1958), pp. 52–53.

[16]Philadelphia Orchestra Association, *Fiftieth Anniversary Season,* p. 25.

[17]Wister, pp. 108–109.

[18]Meuller, p. 129.

[19]Ibid.

[20]Ibid.

[21]Meuller, p. 129.

[22]Digby Baltzell, *Philadelphia Gentlemen: The Making of a National Upper Class* (New York: The Free Press of Glencoe, Inc., 1958), p. 57 and pp. 70–129. Also Meuller, pp. 31–32, 26–29, and 124.

[23]Meuller, p. 129.

[24]Philadelphia Orchestra Association, *Fiftieth Anniversary Season,* p. 15.

[25]Ibid., p. 32.

[26]Ibid., p. 33.

[27]Meuller, p. 130.

[28]"Philadelphia Gold Band is Formed," *North American Magazine,* May 19, 1924, p. 6.

[29]Philadelphia Orchestra Association, *Fiftieth Anniversary Season,* p. 33.

[30]Meuller, p. 127.

[31]"Colorful Maestro Returns," *Philadelphia Sunday Bulletin,* July 17, 1960, p. 14.

[32]Meuller, p. 133.

[33]Philadelphia Orchestra Association, *Fiftieth Anniversary Season,* p. 33. Also see Wister, pp. 23–24, for a more complete resume of programming.

[34]Gerth and Mills, p. 52. "Gift of grace" is the literal translation of charisma.

[35]Ibid., p. 53.

[36]Ibid., p. 53.

[37]"There'll Be No Wage Cut for Stokowski," *Philadelphia*

Record, April 17, 1932, p.(4)a. The breakdown is given as
follows:

49 orchestra concerts	$ 98,000
radio broadcasts	75,000*
Philadelphia Opera Company	10,000
record royalties	20,000*
	$203,000

*These are given as a minimum estimate.

[38]Philadelphia Orchestra Association, *Philadelphia Orchestra
Programs: 1935–36 Season* (Philadelphia: By the Author, 1936).
The shift of power was aided by relegating pro-Stokowski Board
members to an Advisory Board which had no vote.

[39]Established in interviews with Board members and retired
Orchestra members.

[40]Ibid.

[41]Gerth and Mills, pp. 248–249.

[42]Ibid., p. 248. Weber cites the warrior hero as an example.

[43]Gerth and Mills, p. 54.

[44]Ibid.

[45]Ibid., p. 51.

Chapter II

[1]The researching of this phenomenon has taken different forms.
In certain instances the author was personally present. Other
material is derived from interviews and long association with
the principals involved, who include Board members, past and
present Orchestra members, officials of the musicians' union, and
legal counsel. The minutes of Orchestra membership meetings,
union meetings, and the files of the Philadelphia Orchestra Association have been utilized. In order to avoid an endless stream of
footnotes, then, only specific and pertinent sources will be foot-
noted. In addition, because of the prominence of the organization
and many of the individuals who are associated with it, most
interviewees requested anonymity in exchange for frankness, and
are not, therefore, personally identified.

[2]This is confirmed in interviews with present Board members,

one ex-Board member, and the immediate family of a deceased Board member. It is also a widely held assumption among union officials and Orchestra members.

[3]Philadelphia Orchestra Association, *Fiftieth Anniversary Season* (Philadelphia, Pennsylvania: By the Author, 230 South Fifteenth Street, 1950), p. 43.

[4]There was not one Board member interviewed who did not express this sentiment. For example, the author was present at a contract negotiation in 1963 when Board members made a request for an additional ten minutes of allowed concert time because, in order to conform to existing time limitations, Ormandy had had to make some unmusical cuts in compositions performed. When it was pointed out that he could avoid this by simply going slightly overtime, Board members replied that he was so dedicated to the welfare of the institution that he could not bring himself to incur an expenditure by doing this. One Director declared, "He'd come over here and empty the ashtrays if we asked him to."

[5]William H. Whyte, Jr., *The Organization Man* (New York: Simon & Schuster, 1956); and Robert Presthus, *The Organizational Society* (New York: Random House, Inc., 1962), p. 149.

[6]Presthus, p. 131.

[7]Philadelphia Orchestra Association, *Fiftieth Anniversary Season*, pp. 38–39.

[8]Ibid.

[9]Ibid.

[10]Ibid.

[11]Ibid.

[12]Max de Schauensee, "The Music Beat," *Philadelphia Sunday Bulletin*, May 26, 1968, pp. 2, 5.

[13]Philadelphia Orchestra Association, *Fiftieth Anniversary Season*, p. 53.

[14]Ibid.

[15]The Philadelphia Orchestra Association, *The Philadelphia Orchestra* (Concert Program April 6, 7, and 16, 1962).

[16]The Philadelphia Orchestra Association, *Annual Report, 1966–67* and *Annual Report, 1967–68*.

[17]U. S. Congress. House. Subcommittee on Education of the Committee on Education and Labor. *Economic Conditions in the Performing Arts,* 87th cong., 1st and 2nd sess., 1961 and 1962, p. 64.

[18]John Kenneth Galbraith, *The New Industrial State* (Boston: Houghton Mifflin Company, 1967), pp. 6, 211–212.

[19]Chapter I, p. 10.

[20]See Table I–1, p. 12.

[21]"Orchestra Association Disputes Workload Claims," *Philadelphia Evening Bulletin,* November 2, 1966, p. 38.

[22]Philadelphia Orchestra Association, *Fiftieth Anniversary Season,* p. 47.

[23]Ibid., pp. 39–40.

[24]For example, "Wives Dispute Association Claim of 'Easy' Orchestral Life," *Philadelphia Evening Bulletin,* November 10, 1969, Sec. F, p. 41. "Musicians Itemize Their Work Week," *Philadelphia Inquirer,* November 4, 1966, p. 7. "72 Hours A Week —and we mean it!," *Evening Bulletin,* November 4, 1966, p. 24.

[25]Harold C. Schonberg, "Everybody Kissed and Made Up," *New York Times,* January 21, 1968, Sec. D, p. 17.

[26]"The Lost Accord," *Philadelphia Magazine,* December, 1966, p. 78.

[27]Presthus, pp. 25–26.

[28]Philadelphia Orchestra Association, *Fiftieth Anniversary Season,* p. 47.

[29]Ibid.

[30]Ibid.

[31]"Orchestra Bares Its Finances, Girds for $10 Million Campaign," *Philadelphia Evening Bulletin,* March 18, 1968, p. 1.

[32]Interview with John Healy, consultant to the Philadelphia Orchestra Association for the Philadelphia Orchestra Challenge Program, Philadelphia, Pennsylvania, December 8, 1968.

[33]Interview with Julian Goldberk, former counsel for the Philadelphia Orchestra members, Philadelphia, Pennsylvania, September 3, 1961, and Bernard Katz, former counsel for the Philadelphia Orchestra members, Philadelphia, Pennsylvania, September 26, 1966.

[34]Carl Dreyfuss, "Prestige Grading: A Mechanism of Control," *Reader in Bureaucracy*, ed. Robert K. Merton, Ailsa P. Gray, Barbara Hockey, and Hanan C. Selvin (New York: The Free Press, 1952), p. 258.

[35]The Boston Symphony Orchestra has made provisions in its latest contract for standardized promotional procedures in the string section.

[36]"The Lost Accord," *Philadelphia Magazine*, December, 1966, pp. 86–87.

[37]Ibid.

[38]Ibid.

[39]Ibid.

[40]G. A. Brakeley & Company, Inc., "A Fund-Raising Study for the Philadelphia Orchestra Challenge Program" (Philadelphia, Pennsylvania: By the Author, 1967), p. 11.

[41]The Philadelphia Orchestra Challenge Program was launched under the impetus of a two million dollar grant by the Ford Foundation which required that the Association raise four million dollars in matching funds.

[42]Philadelphia Orchestra Association, *Fiftieth Anniversary Season*, pp. 54–55.

[43]Ibid.

[44]Ibid.

[45]G. A. Brakeley & Company, Inc., p. 5.

[46]Ibid.

[47]Ibid.

Chapter III

[1]Harold D. Lasswell and Abraham Kaplan, *Power and Society* (New Haven and London: Yale University Press, 1950), p. 87.

[2]Edward C. Banfield and James Q. Wilson, *City Politics* (New York: Random House, 1963), pp. 248–250.

[3]Baltzell, p. 57.

[4]This emerges in interviews with all segments of the Philadelphia community. Also see: Baltzell, p. 366; "Off the Cuff," *Philadelphia Magazine*, February, 1967, p. 23; Philadelphia

Orchestra Association, *Fiftieth Anniversary*, p. 12. This describes the first Philadelphia Orchestra concert as a "brilliant social gathering," and contains a newspaper quote to the effect that, "This is a new combination, originated by a few—millionaires— to prepare for 'licking Boston'."

[5]Baltzell, p. 32.

[6]Ibid., p. 5.

[7]Ibid., p. 7.

[8]Ibid., pp. 65–66.

[9]William Domhoff, *Who Rules America?* (Englewood Cliffs: Prentice-Hall, Inc., 1967), pp. 13–14, quoting Dixon Wecter, *The Saga of American Society* (New York: Charles Scribner's & Sons) and Cleveland Amory, *Who Killed Society?* (New York: Harper & Bros., 1960). Also see Baltzell, p. 8 and p. 20, in which he quotes Ferdinand Lundberg, *America's 60 Families* and Gustave Meyers, *History of the Great American Fortunes*.

[10]Baltzell, p. 19.

[11]This is established in interviews with the Orchestra manager and other staff of the Association. Also see "The Lost Accord," *Philadelphia Magazine*, December, 1966, p. 79. In this article one Board member is quoted as follows: "You could be on the Board and live and die and never know what's going on."

[12]Philadelphia Orchestra Association, *The Philadelphia Orchestra* (Concert Program, March 24, 1967), p. 26.

[13]Ibid.

[14]G. A. Brakeley & Company, Inc., p. 26.

[15]"Off the Cuff," *Philadelphia Magazine*, February, 1967, p. 24. This opinion was also expressed by Duffield to the author in January, 1967 and to a meeting of the Orchestra members on March 8, 1967.

[16]"Orchestra Unit Plans to Add 12 Directors," *Philadelphia Inquirer*, December 17, 1966, p. 14.

[17]Ibid.

[18]Ibid.

[19]G. A. Brakeley & Company, Inc.

[20]Ibid., pp. 8–9.

[21]Interview with Digby Baltzell, Philadelphia, Pennsylvania, September, 1968.

[22]Baltzell, p. 5. Also see, for example, Phyllis Feldkamp, "Music and Vintage Mink Every Friday," *Philadelphia Sunday Bulletin,* January 12, 1969, Section 4, p. 6.

[23]Labor lawyers and mediators who deal in the area of non-profit organizations have substantiated this. One federal mediator told the author that this phenomenon is particularly prevalent on hospital boards.

[24]One observer at the 1966 labor negotiations has reported that this was a constant reaction of both the President and Chairman of the Board. They particularly resented any implication that they derived a psychic or social benefit from their offices. When it was pointed out to them how hard the Orchestra members worked, they constantly pointed out that they themselves worked without any compensation whatever.

[25]See the evaluation of programming for the Ormandy era in Table II–1, Chapter II, p. 28.

[26]G. A. Brakely & Company, Inc., pp. 9–10.

[27]Philadelphia Orchestra Association, *Fiftieth Anniversary Season,* pp. 54–55.

[28]"The Lost Accord," *Philadelphia Magazine,* December, 1966, p. 90. Also see Martin Mayer, "Managing Orchestras is a Fine Art Too," Fortune (September 1, 1968). Mayer brings out that fund drives are often conducted by upper class women's committees which tend to contact only their own friends.

[29]G. A. Brakeley & Company, Inc., pp. 4–5. This report points out the widespread recognition on the part of the community of the value to it of the Philadelphia Orchestra. The whole tenor of the section entitled "Positive Factors" is that there exists great latent financial support for the Orchestra in the community. Representatives of both organized labor and city government have told the author that their organizations would substantially support the Orchestra in return for Board representation.

[30]Participants in labor negotiations and day-to-day labor relations with the Board, including the author, have been constantly struck by the Board's attitude that the musicians are somehow

very greedy people because they constantly seek material returns from an endeavor which the Board regards as a labor of love. The musicians hence become people from whom the organization must be protected.

Chapter IV

[1]In 1948, during one such dispute, the Board took an unprecedented action which demonstrates the bitterness of the conflict. It announced publicly that the 1948–49 concert season would not go on—in effect, cancelling all subscriptions and releasing all the musicians from their contracts—because it felt that the wage demands of the musicians would "seriously impair the finances of the organization." The Board was not bluffing. Staff people later confirmed that they were in the process of returning subscription monies when the strike collapsed.

[2]Philadelphia Orchestra members' committee files. See also, "Musicians Ask Right to Fire Conductor," *New York Times*, April 27, 1963, p. 15:1.

[3]Ibid.

[4]Minutes of the Philadelphia Orchestra membership meetings reveal that these proposals had substantial membership support. They were overwhelmingly approved at a membership meeting, 78 to 12.

[5]This did result in increased militancy on the part of the union. The length of the 1966 strike was partially attributable to this factor.

[6]ICSOM did win from the national office of the American Federation of Musicians the right for symphonic musicians to be present as observers during the negotiations for a new national recording agreement in 1964, and this led to a formula whereby the musicians came to share in record royalty payments which had been going exclusively to the union.

[7]"Philadelphia Musicians Plan Vote on Conductor Clause," *New York Times*, May 1, 1963, p. 34:7.

[8]Three Board members, in separate interviews, voiced the same

sentiment to the effect that this event made them realize how deep the discontent in the Orchestra must have been.

[9]U. S. Congress. House. Subcommittee on Education of the Committee on Education and Labor. "Economic Conditions in the Performing Arts," 87th Congress, 1st and 2nd sess., 1961 and 1962, pp. 53–60. The testimony of Roger Hall, manager of the Philadelphia Orchestra, was so apprehensive of government intervention in the arts to better economic conditions for performers that he was chided by Representative Thompson. In an interview in September of 1968, the President of the Association declared his complete opposition to government subsidy of the arts. A survey of symphonic boards of directors by the American Symphony Orchestra League disclosed that they were overwhelmingly opposed to such a development.

[10]Shortly after signing the 1963 contract, the Association granted substantial increases to most first chair players, many of whom had not even asked for an increase and whose contracts had additional years to run.

[11]C. Wanton Balis, Jr., President of the Philadelphia Orchestra Association, and Charles Musumecci, President of Local 77, American Federation of Musicians, "Philadelphia Orchestra Association Agreement," September 9, 1963.

[12]"Musicians Negotiate Own Contract," AFL–CIO News, October 5, 1963, p. 4.

[13]Ibid.

[14]Ibid.

[15]Ibid.

[16]Leon E. Lunden, "Bargaining Prospects for Major Symphony Orchestras," Monthly Labor Review, May, 1966, p. 482.

[17]Alvin Toffler, The Culture Consumers (New York: St. Martin's Press, 1964), pp. 131–132.

[18]A petition was circulated at Interlochen, Michigan, in August of 1963; and the election was held at Salt Lake City, Utah, about two weeks later. The Orchestra members' attorney had advised by telephone that the Orchestra take no action while on tour because he felt that people think better in a familiar environ-

ment rather than in a situation such as a tour where there is emotional strain. The opposition, however, realized this also and undoubtedly wanted to take advantage of the fact that the Interlochen Festival involved a labor dispute and feeling, at the moment, was running high.

[19]"Flying the Coop," *Time,* October 7, 1966, pp. 54–56.

[20]Patrick Douglas, "The Symphony vs The University," *Seattle Magazine* (Vol. III, No. 33, December, 1966), pp. 50–57.

[21]George Rochberg, "Contemporary Music in an Affluent Society," *ASCAP Today* (Vol. I, No. 3, Autumn, 1967), p. 10.

[22]"The Lost Accord," *Philadelphia Magazine,* December, 1966, p. 91.

[23]William G. Scott, *Organization Theory* (Homewood, Illinois: Richard D. Irwin, Inc., 1967), pp. 34–35.

[24]Elton Mayo, *The Human Problems of an Industrial Civilization* (New York: The MacMillan Co., 2nd ed., 1946).

[25]Scott, pp. 34–35. Chris Argyris is a leading spokesman for the Industrial Humanism Movement, which postulates individual needs as the starting point of organization theory. In an article entitled, "We Must Make Work Worthwhile," *Life Magazine* (May 5, 1967), p. 56, he points out that work which requires more passivity than activity, more submissiveness than responsibility, more surface abilities than complex and deeper activities is "better suited to the world of infants than the world of adults." He further contends that attempting to convince the worker that his job is very important, even when only a small part of a larger whole, is ineffective. Under such conditions, the worker withdraws and limits his work involvement because he perceives this as a means of maintaining self-esteem while continuing to produce. This, however, is self-defeating and actually damaging to confidence and self-esteem. His focus becomes stronger upon wages and working conditions than upon self-realization. Argyris declares: "Once he accomplishes this, even increased benefits as a reward for productivity lose their power. Instead they become more compensation for his dissatisfaction."

Douglas McGregor, another Industrial Humanist, also views egoistic needs as a primary work motivation. In his book, *The*

Human Side of Enterprise (New York:McGraw-Hill Book Co., 1960), pp. 38–39, he declares these needs to be: (1) Self-Esteem (self-respect, confidence, autonomy, achievement, competence, knowledge); (2) Reputation (status, recognition, appreciation, respect); (3) Self-Fulfillment (realizing of potentialities, continued self-development, creativity). McGregor contends that lack of status can result in a sickness of behavior which is not indicative of human nature but of the deprivation of an egoistic need. He feels that the average person holds no inherent dislike of work, but that his view of it as satisfaction or punishment is dependent upon external conditions.

Industrial Humanism views the hierarchy of needs as an ascending progression. As Love, Safety, and Security needs are met, they cease to act as motivators and the worker turns toward higher needs of creativity and self-fulfillment.

[26]Erich Fromm, *The Sane Society* (New York: Rinehart & Co., 1955), p. 29.

[27]Ibid., pp. 112–113.

[28]Ibid., p. 125.

[29]Ibid., pp. 177–178.

[30]Ibid., pp. 180–181.

[31]Ibid., p. 182.

[32]Charles R. Walker and R. H. Guest, *The Man on the Assembly Line* (Cambridge, Massachusetts: Harvard University Press, 1952), pp. 142–143.

[33]Fromm, pp. 289–290.

[34]M. S. Viteles, *Motivation and Morale in Industry* (New York: W. W. Norton & Co., 1953), pp. 49–50, from Fromm, pp. 290–292.

[35]William J. Goode and Irving Fowler, "Incentive Factors in a Low Morale Plant," *American Sociological Review* (1949), pp. 618–624, from Scott, p. 289.

[36]Daniel Katz, Nathan Maccoby, and Nancy C. Morse, "Productivity, Supervision, and Morale in an Office Situation," *Institute for Social Research* (1950), p. 63, from Scott, p. 289.

[37]J. F. Lincoln, *Incentive Management* (Cleveland, Ohio: Lincoln Electric Company, 1951) from Fromm, pp. 113–114.

[38]Bernard Berelson and Gary Steiner, Human Behavior: *An*

Inventory of Scientific Findings (New York: Harcourt, Brace, & World, Inc., 1964), p. 369 and pp. 404–405.

[39]Curtis Institute of Music, *Catalogue, 1966–67* (Philadelphia, Pennsylvania: By the Author, 18th and Locust Streets, 1966).

[40]Philadelphia Musical Academy, *Catalogue, 1965–66* (Philadelphia, Pennsylvania: By the Author, 1617 Spruce Street, 1965).

[41]Interview with Erich Leinsdorf, conductor of the Boston Symphony, New York City, December, 1966. Interview with George Rochberg, former Chairman of the Music Department of the University of Pennsylvania, Philadelphia, Pennsylvania, October, 1968. Also see, "The Lost Accord," *Philadelphia Magazine,* December, 1966, in which Henry Schmidt, former Personnel Manager of the Philadelphia Orchestra, is quoted as follows: "The kids who've come out of Curtis and Juilliard today are all disappointed soloists."

[42]Interview with George Zazofsky, member of the Boston Symphony Orchestra and Chairman of the International Conference of Symphony and Opera Musicians (ICSOM), Philadelphia, Pennsylvania, November, 1965. Interview with Joseph Castaldo, President of the Philadelphia Musical Academy, Philadelphia, Pennsylvania, October, 1968. Interview with Boris Sokoloff, manager of the Philadelphia Orchestra, Philadelphia, Pennsylvania, October, 1968.

[43]Berelson and Steiner, p. 369.

[44]Interview with Dr. Bernard Borislow, Consulting Psychologist, Philadelphia, Pennsylvania, March, 1967.

[45]See footnote 37.

[46]"Music," *Newsweek*, September 5, 1966, p. 80.

[47]The manipulative nature of this relationship was touched upon in the analysis of recording procedures in Chapter II. It was pointed out that it was to the financial interest of the conductor and the Association to speed up the recording sessions and that, when the conductor did this, the men became embittered.

[48]McGregor, p. 27.

[49]Charles Blackman, *Behind the Baton* (New York: Charos Enterprises, Inc., 1964).

[50]Ibid., pp. 105–106.

[51]Emily Coleman, *New York Times,* April 2, 1967, p. 27, quoting Zubin Mehta, conductor of the Los Angeles Philharmonic Orchestra.

[52]Toffler, p. 133.

[53]Blackman, p. 102.

[54]For a good exposition of how aggressions generated by lower level supervision are projected into labor relations on a higher level against management, see Robert N. McMurray, "the Clinical Psychology Approach," *Psychology of Labor-Management Relations,* Industrial Relations Research Association, Proceedings of meeting (Denver Colorado: September 7, 1949), p. 72.

[55]Scott, p. 79.

[56]Ibid., p. 78.

[57]Leon Festinger and Elliot Aronson, "The Arousal and Reduction of Dissonance in Social Contexts," in *Group Dynamics Research Theory,* 2nd ed., Doran Cartwright and Alvin Zander (Evanston, Illinois: Row Peterson Company, 1960), p. 218.

[58]Interview with Dr. Bernard Borislow, Philadelphia, Pennsylvania, March, 1967.

[59]Scott, p. 79.

[60]Some of the opportunities which arose to discard the requirement of working year-round which the Orchestra members showed no inclination to utilize were: (1) In the process of preparing for collective bargaining for the following contract (1966–67), the Orchestra committee collected over 200 unsigned proposals from the membership, none of which contained any suggestion of reducing the contract to anything less than 52 weeks. (2) At a membership meeting on October 23, 1964, a motion was made and seconded that the third year of the existing contract, which was to initiate the 52-week concept, be cancelled. The meeting adjourned with little discussion and no request for a vote, and at the following meeting on October 26, the motion was withdrawn. (3) At an Orchestra members' meeting during the 1965–66 season, which was called for the purpose of drawing up and discussing demands for the upcoming contract negotiations, an offer was submitted by a representative of the

Robin Hood Dell management to induce the Orchestra members to conclude a separate contract covering the summer period of the Dell concerts. This would have made these weeks optional for each individual Orchestra member, and, in effect, have foreclosed the possibility of renewing the 52-week formula with the Philadelphia Orchestra Association. The offer was tabled and never brought to the floor. (4) Subsequently, when the Association offered an individual option of taking off the Dell season without salary, there were only six applications.

[61]Chris Argyris, "We Must Make Work Worthwhile," *Life,* May 5, 1967, p. 56.

[62]For an excellent study of this phenomenon as manifested in Japanese-Americans in a relocation camp during World War II, see Alexander Leighton, *The Governing of Men* (Princeton: Princeton University Press, 1945).

[63]Cartwright and Zander, pp. 170–171.

[64]Scott, p. 212.

[65]Cartwright and Zander, p. 492.

[66]McGregor, pp. 38–39.

[67]Cartwright and Zander, p. 539. Lewin, Lippit, and White, in experiments with different groups under Autocratic, Democratic, and Laissez-Faire leadership, found the last two superior to Autocracy, but Laissez-Faire to be less organized, less efficient, and less satisfactory than Democracy. "The lack of active guiding suggestions in Laissez-Faire often resulted in disorganization and in failure and setbacks." They also found a tendency to confuse Laissez-Faire with Democracy. This explains the new Orchestra members' committee statement to the effect that they would be a "democratic" committee by making no recommendations.

[68]The pathological quality of this situation is illustrated by the fact that the Orchestra members specifically directed their committee not to meet with the Board while at the same time there were complaints by the Orchestra members that the Board would not meet with their committee.

[69]Berelson and Steiner, p. 331. When labor-management conflict intensifies, leaders will avoid contact with employers in fear

of member criticism. The reduced communication and interaction in turn gives further impetus to an escalation of conflict.

[70]Jack R. Gibb, "Defensive Communications" *Journal of Communication,* Vol. XI, No. 3, September, 1963. Gibb finds that in a situation where people perceive themselves as threatened they will begin to behave defensively, and that such behavior inhibits communication and the correct choice of solutions.

Mattie Kibrick Gershenfeld, "Factors Affecting Responsible Behavior under Conditions of Threat and Non-Threat" (unpublished doctoral dissertation, Temple University, 1967). This study was able to demonstrate that under conditions of perceived threat there is a reduced ability to deal with problems and find creative solutions.

[71]Interview with three members of the 1963 Philadelphia Orchestra members' committee, Leonard Hale, Jerome, Wigler, and Bert Phillips, Philadelphia, Pennsylvania, January, 1965.

[72]*Minutes of Meetings,* Philadelphia Orchestra members' committee.

[73]Interview with three members of the 1963 Philadelphia Orchestra members' committee, Leonard Hale, Jerome Wigler, and Bert Phillips, Philadelphia, Pennsylvania, January, 1955. This was confirmed in an interview with Joseph Santarlasci, assistant manager of the Philadelphia Orchestra, Philadelphia, Pennsylvania, December, 1967. Mr. Santarlasci said that he was instructed by the President of the Association to keep a week of the Orchestra schedule free in the Spring of 1966 in anticipation of a week's vacation for the Orchestra members as settlement of the Saratoga issue. Concerts for this week were eventually scheduled only six weeks in advance when it became apparent that no settlement with the Orchestra members would take place in time to utilize it. This is further confirmed by the printed date book issued to Orchestra members in September of 1965, which showed a blank week in the Spring of 1965.

[74]*Minutes of Meetings,* Philadelphia Orchestra members' committee, October 21, 1964 to August 19, 1966. There were a total of 26 meetings during this period in which the subject was

considered and the body was unable to agree upon even a first step toward resolution.

[75]Ibid., March 16, 1965. The President of Local 77, American Federation of Musicians, came to the Academy of Music and made a personal plea to the Orchestra members to negotiate the issue.

[76]Ibid., March 12, 1965.

[77]Another example of this malaise was the demand by Orchestra members that an individual option of rail rather than air travel, which had applied to domestic tours, should also apply to a projected tour of South America. The Orchestra members predictably lost out on this obviously impossible demand (the entire tour was five weeks and it would have taken almost that long to reach South America by train, if that were indeed possible), but not before they had gone through an arbitration procedure and a subsequent appeal to a federal court. Needless to say, mutual hostility was increased even more by this episode.

[78]Board members expressed fears to mediators involved in the negotiations that the leadership of the Orchestra members was too irrational to negotiate. One Board member was convinced of a subversive plot during the strike. Another, perhaps with the clearest insight of all, pointed out that the leaders of the Orchestra members had struck such a militant posture and fanned the flames of hatred so high that they were now unable to negotiate because anything less than the complete surrender of the Board would have left them to face the wrath of their own people.

[79]G. A. Brakeley & Company, Inc., *A Fund-Raising Study for the Philadelphia Orchestra Challenge Program* (Philadelphia, Pennsylvania: By the Author, 1967), p. 5.

[80]Interview with Seymour Rosen, former Secretary of the American Symphony Orchestra League, Philadelphia, Pennsylvania, December, 1967.

[81]Ibid. The 1948–49 season was almost cancelled by a labor dispute. The 1943–44 season started with one rehearsal for the opening concert because of a contract dispute. There were strikes in 1954, 1959, 1961, and 1966, the last being the longest in symphonic history. In addition, tours to the Soviet Union and

South America were originally cancelled in labor disputes, although the Orchestra did get to these places at a later date.

[82]This is not to say that the expiration of every contract will be the signal for another strike. Factors may militate against control of the group by the most-alienated. For example, the lawyer who last represented the Orchestra members seemed to wield some influence over them. Last year, at his recommendation, the Orchestra members' committee went back to face-to-face negotiations with the Board and consummated a new contract in a conciliatory manner. This was probably also due to the fact that the Orchestra members were not anxious for another strike. The 1966 strike was a costly one for them and they did not achieve their objectives. The major effort of that strike was to dislodge the Board and form a new Association. This failed. The economic gains were marginal and the Philadelphia Orchestra fell behind the other major symphonies for the first time. The whole experience had a cathartic effect which tended to dilute militancy for awhile. Another factor may have been some new Board members who convinced the Orchestra members to give them a chance to build better relations. The most-alienated group remains, however, and its influence is admitted by committee members. Recently the Orchestra members' committee had to appeal to the union to stop certain Orchestra members from spreading charges that the committee was in collusion with the management because they were meeting with the Board in a labor relations committee. The most-alienated group numbers variously between 25 and 40 individuals. In the ratification vote on the last contract, therefore, the negative vote of 34 strongly suggests its continuing existence.

[83]Circulars were distributed on the picket line to the public which implied that the Association leadership did not really care about the organization. See, for example, "The Lost Accord," *Philadelphia Magazine,* December, 1966, in which Orchestra members see the leadership of the Association as authoritarian and cruel, and in which charges are made of dishonest bookkeeping.

[84]G. A. Brakeley & Co., pp. 11–12, 19–20.

[85]Ibid., p. 26.

[86]There is another situation which deserves mention here which poses a threat to the long term existence of symphonic organizations and which may be related to the problem of bureaucratization and the lack of opportunity for individual fulfillment, although there is not sufficient evidence at the present time to establish a direct causal relationship. At the present time a serious shortage of good string players is threatening even the major symphony orchestras, according to Mason Jones, personnel manager of the Philadelphia Orchestra. For example, an examination of sample issues of the *International Musician,* the official organ of the American Federation of Musicians, reveals the reversal from surplus to shortage which has taken place in this category since World War II. In 1932 and again in 1939, a random sampling of issues reveals large numbers of "At Liberty" advertisements by string players, and no "Help Wanted" notices from symphony orchestras. In contrast, in 1968, there are no string players advertising for jobs, but rather "Help Wanted" notices from major orchestras as the San Francisco Symphony, the Philadelphia Orchestra, the Boston Symphony, and the Cincinnati Symphony. Many people in the field, including Erich Leinsdorf of the Boston Symphony and Zubin Mehta of the Los Angeles Philharmonic, feel that the lack of opportunity for individual fulfillment in a symphony orchestra is a strong causative factor. The author has spoken to many string students, particularly those highly talented people who are to be found at the Curtis Institute of Music, and many have confirmed this.

Chapter V

[1]Interview with Joseph Castaldo, composer and President of the Philadelphia Musical Academy, Philadelphia, Pennsylvania, September, 1968.

Interview with George Rochberg, composer and former Chairman of the Music Department of the University of Pennsylvania, Philadelphia, Pennsylvania, September, 1968.

Interview with Daniel Webster, music critic with the *Philadelphia Inquirer,* Philadelphia, Pennsylvania, September, 1968.

See statement by Anshel Brusilow, conductor and former concert-master of the Philadelphia Orchestra, in "The Lost Accord," *Philadelphia Magazine,* December, 1966.

Paul Hume, Lukas Foss, Elliott Carter, and Leon Kirchner, "The Symphony: Is It Alive? Or Just Embalmed?" *New York Times,* September 22, 1968, p. 25.

[2]Castaldo, Rochberg, and Brusilow all agreed upon this.

[3]Professional copyists' fees for master scores are about $5 per page. The average cost of a master score for a composition for full symphony orchestra runs about $2,000. The result is that unless a grant is forthcoming, many composers cannot afford to produce a master score, without which many conductors will not give them an evaluation or consideration for performance.

[4]Hume *et al.,* p. 25.

[5]Ibid.

[6]In addition to the resistance of the leadership to experimentation or innovation, there are other barriers to the use of the Orchestra in small groups. The members of the Orchestra, for example, fear that the management will exploit them unfairly and increase preferential treatment for favored players by allocating choice assignments. Some Orchestra members, whose playing is not of the best quality, fear exposure in small groups. The union is also opposed to the concept because it fears that the Association would try to absorb work which is presently performed by other small groups of union members in Philadelphia. Conductors are also reluctant, in many cases, to undertake the difficult task of learning the new music.

[7]Hume *et al.,* p. 25.

[8]George Rochberg, "Contemporary Music in an Affluent Society," *ASCAP Today,* Vol. I, No. 3 (Autumn, 1967), p. 10.

[9]Ibid.

[10]Ibid.

[11]Hume *et al.,* p. 25.

[12]Ibid.

[13]Rochberg.

[14]"What's Happened to the Audience?", *New York Times,* December 21, 1968, p. 48:1.

[15]Ibid.

[16]Ibid.

[17]Abram Chasins, "The Rise and Decline of the Boston Symphony Orchestra," *McCalls* (March, 1969), p. 34.

[18]"Orchestra Appoints New Manager," *Philadelphia Inquirer,* July 5, 1964, p. 37.

[19]William J. Baumol and William G. Bowen, *Performing Arts: The Economic Dilemma* (New York: The Twentieth Century Fund, 1966), pp. 387–407.

[20]Ibid., pp. 95–96.

[21]Ibid., p. 328.

[22]James Felton, "Big Orchestras Face Extinction, Philadelphia Music Backer Says," *Philadelphia Evening Bulletin,* December 29, 1966, p. 32.

[23]Baumol and Bowen, pp. 345–346.

[24]Ibid., p. 333.

[25]Richard F. Shepard, "Ford Fund Glum On Arts Outlook," *New York Times,* March 2, 1969, p. 47.

[26]Harold Schonberg, "Music," *New York Times,* December 4, 1966, Section II, p. 23.

[27]James Felton, "Giant Financial Woes Plague Big Orchestras," *Philadelphia Evening Bulletin,* June 29, 1969, TJ p. 2.

[28]In Philadelphia, for example, two recent concerts of Mahler's music at the Electric Factory, a psychedelic music center, drew large numbers of enthusiastic young listeners. The same phenomenon has been reported from New York.

Bibliography

BOOKS

Amory, Cleveland. *Who Killed Society?* New York: Harper & Brothers, 1960.

Baltzell, Digby. *Philadelphia Gentlemen: The Making of a National Upper Class.* New York: The Free Press of Glencoe, Inc., 1958.

Banfield, Edward C., and James Q. Wilson. *City Politics.* New York: Random House, 1963.

Baumol, William J., and William G. Bowen. *Performing Arts: The Economic Dilemma.* New York: Twentieth Century Fund, 1966.

Berelson, Bernard and Gary Steiner. *Human Behavior: An Inventory of Scientific Findings.* New York: Harcourt, Brace & World, Inc., 1964.

Blackman, Charles. *Behind the Baton.* New York: Charos Enterprises, Inc., 1964.

Domhoff, William. *Who Rules America?* Englewood Cliffs, N. J.: Prentice-Hall, Inc., 1967.

Dreyfuss, Carl. "Prestige Grading: A Mechanism of Control," *Reader in Bureaucracy.* Edited by Robert K. Merton, Ailsa P. Gray, Barbara Hockey, and Hanan C. Selvin. New York: The Free Press, 1952.

Festinger, Leon and Elliot Aronson. "The Arousal and Reduction of Dissonance in Social Contexts," in *Group Dynamics Research Theory,* 2nd ed., Dorin Cartwright and Alvin Zander. Evanston, Illinois: Row Peterson Company, 1960.

Fromm, Erich. *The Sane Society.* New York: Rinehart & Company, 1955.

Galbraith, John Kenneth. *The New Industrial State.* Boston: Houghton Mifflin Company, 1967.

Gerth, H. H. and C. Wright Mills. *From Max Weber: Essays in Sociology.* New York and London: Oxford University Press, 1958.

Lasswell, Harold D. and Abraham Kaplan. *Power and Society*. New Haven and London: Yale University Press, 1950.

Leighton, Alexander. *The Governing of Men*. Princeton: Princeton University Press, 1945.

Lincoln, J. F. *Incentive Management*. Cleveland, Ohio: Lincoln Electric Company, 1951.

Mayo, Elton. *The Human Problems of an Industrial Civilization*. New York: The MacMillan Company, 2nd ed., 1946.

McGregor, Douglas. *The Human Side of Enterprise*. New York: McGraw-Hill Book Company, 1960.

Meuller, John H. *The American Symphony Orchestra*. Bloomington: Indiana University Press, 1951.

Presthus, Robert. *The Organizational Society*. New York: Random House, Inc., 1962.

Scott, William G. *Organization Theory*. Homewood, Illinois: Richard D. Irwin, Inc., 1967.

Toffler, Alvin. *The Culture Consumers*. New York: St. Martin's Press, 1964.

Viteles, M. S. *Motivation and Morale in Industry*. New York: W. W. Norton & Company, 1953.

Walker, Charles R. and R. H. Guest. *The Man on the Assembly Line*. Cambridge, Massachusetts: Harvard University Press, 1952.

Whyte, William H. Jr. *The Organization Man*. New York: Simon & Schuster, 1956.

Wister, Frances Anne. *Twenty-Five Years of the Philadelphia Orchestra*. Philadelphia: Philadelphia Women's Committees for the Philadelphia Orchestra, 1925.

PUBLIC DOCUMENTS

U. S. Congress. House. Subcommittee on Education of the Committee on Education and Labor. *Economic Conditions in the Performing Arts*, 87th cong., 1st and 2nd sess., 1961 and 1962.

ARTICLES AND PERIODICALS

Argyris, Chris. "We Must Make Work Worthwhile," *Life*, May 5, 1967, 56.

Chasins, Abram. "The Rise and Decline of the Boston Symphony Orchestra," *McCalls*, March, 1969, 34.

Coleman, Emily. *New York Times*, April 2, 1967, 27.

"Colorful Maestro Returns," *Philadelphia Sunday Bulletin,* July 17, 1960, 14.

de Schauensee, Max. "The Music Beat," *Philadelphia Sunday Bulletin,* May 26, 1968, 2, 5.

Douglas, Patrick. "The Symphony vs The University," *Seattle Magazine,* Vol. III, No. 33 (December, 1966), 50–57.

Feldkamp, Phyllis. "Music and Vintage Mink Every Friday," *Philadelphia Sunday Bulletin,* January 12, 1969, Sec. 4, 6.

Felton, James. "Big Orchestras Face Extinction, Philadelphia Music Backer Says," *Philadelphia Evening Bulletin,* December 29, 1966, 32.

Felton, James. "Giant Financial Woes Plague Big Orchestras," *Philadelphia Evening Bulletin,* June 29, 1969, TJ p. 2.

"Flying the Coop," *Times,* October 7, 1966, 54–56.

Gibb, Jack R. "Defensive Communications," *Journal of Communication,* Vol. XI, No. 3 (September, 1963).

Goode, William J. and Irving Fowler. "Incentive Factors in a Low Morale Plant, *American Sociological Review* (1949), 618–624.

Hune, Paul, Lukas Foss, Elliot Carter, and Elliot Kirchner. "The Symphony: Is It Alive? Or Just Embalmed?" *New York Times,* September 22, 1968, 25.

Katz, Daniel, Nathan Maccoby, and Nancy Morse. "Productivity Supervision and Morale in an Office Situation," *Institute for Social Research* (1950), 63.

"The Lost Accord," *Philadelphia Magazine,* December, 1966, 78, 86–87, 90, 91.

Lunden, Leon E. "Bargaining Prospects for Major Symphony Orchestras," *Monthly Labor Review,* May, 1966, 482.

Mayer, Martin. "Managing Orchestra is a Fine Art Too," *Fortune,* September 1, 1968.

"Music," *Newsweek,* September 5, 1966, 80.

"Musicians Ask Right to Fire Conductor," *New York Times,* April 27, 1963, 15:1.

"Musicians Itemize Their Work Week," *Philadelphia Inquirer,* November 4, 1966, 7.

"Musicians Negotiate Own Contract," *AFL-CIO News,* October 5, 1963, 4.

"Off the Cuff," *Philadelphia Magazine,* February, 1967, 23, 24.

"Orchestra Appoints New Manager," *Philadelphia Inquirer,* July 5, 1964, 37.

"Orchestra Association Disputes Workload Claims," *Philadelphia Evening Bulletin,* November 2, 1966, 38.

"Orchestra Bares Its Finances, Girds for $10 Million Campaign," *Philadelphia Evening Bulletin,* March 18, 1968, 1.

"Orchestra Unit Plans to Add 12 Directors," *Philadelphia Inquirer,* December 17, 1966, 14.

"Philadelphia Gold Band Is Formed," *North American Magazine,* May 19, 1924, 6.

"Philadelphia Musicians Plan Vote on Conductor Clause," *New York Times,* May 1, 1963, 34:7.

Rochberg, George. "Contemporary Music in an Affluent Society," *ASCAP Today,* Vol. I, No. 3 (Autumn, 1967), 10.

Schonberg, Harold C. "Music," *New York Times,* December 4, 1966, Sec. II, p. 23.

Schonberg, Harold C. "Everybody Kissed and Made Up," *New York Times,* January 21, 1968, Sec. D, p. 17.

"72 Hours A Week—and we mean it!" *Philadelphia Evening Bulletin,* November 4, 1966, 24.

Shepard, Richard F. "Ford Fund Glum On Arts Outlook," *New York Times,* March 2, 1969, 47.

"There'll Be No Wage Cut for Stokowski," *Philadelphia Record,* April 17, 1932, (4)a.

"What's Happened to the Audience?" *New York Times,* December 21, 1968, 48:1.

"Wives Dispute Association Claim of 'Easy' Orchestral Life," *Philadelphia Evening Bulletin,* November 10, 1966, Sec. F, p. 41.

REPORTS

Balis, C. Wanton Jr., President of the Philadelphia Orchestra Association and Musumeci, Charles, President of Local 77, American Federation of Musicians. "Philadelphia Orchestra Association Agreement," September 9, 1963.

Curtis Institute of Music. *Catalogue, 1966–67.* Philadelphia, Pennsylvania: By the Author, 18th & Locust Streets, 1966.

McMurray, Robert N. "The Clinical Psychology Approach," *Psychology of Labor-Management Relations,* Industrial Relations Research Association, Proceedings of meeting. Denver, Colorado: September 7, 1949.

Philadelphia Musical Academy. *Catalogue, 1965–66.* Philadelphia, Pennsylvania: By the Author, 1617 Spruce Street, 1965.

The Philadelphia Orchestra Association. *Annual Report, 1966–67.*
The Philadelphia Orchestra Association. *Annual Report, 1967–68.*
Philadelphia Orchestra Association. *Fiftieth Anniversary Season.* Phila-
    delphia, Pennsylvania: By the Author, 230 S. 15th Street, 1950.
The Philadelphia Orchestra Association. *The Philadelphia Orchestra.*
    Concert Program, April 6, 7 and 16, 1962.
Philadelphia Orchestra Association. *The Philadelphia Orchestra.* Con-
    cert Program, March 24, 1967.
Philadelphia Orchestra Association. *Philadelphia Orchestra Programs:
    1935–36 Season.* Philadelphia: By the Author, 1936.

UNPUBLISHED MATERIAL

Brakeley, G. A., & Company, Inc. "A Fund-Raising Study for the
    Philadelphia Orchestra Challenge Program." Philadelphia, Pennsyl-
    vania: By the Author, 1967.
Gershenfeld, Mattie Kibrick. "Factors Affecting Responsible Behavior
    Under Conditions of Threat and Non-Threat," unpublished doctoral
    dissertation, Temple University, 1967.
Philadelphia Orchestra members' committee files.
Philadelphia Orchestra members' committee. *Minutes of Meetings.*
Philadelphia Orchestra members' committee. *Minutes of Meetings,*
    October 21, 1964 to August 19, 1966.

OTHER SOURCES

American Federation of Musicians, Local 77, Philadelphia, Pennsyl-
    vania. Interviews and discussions with the following officials: Romeo
    Cella, A. A. Tomei, Charles McConnell, Ray Hyman, Don Diogenia,
    Charles Musumecci, Lee Herman, Fred Calabrese, Anthony Cuci-
    notta, James DeFranco. September, 1951 to August, 1967.
Curtis Institute of Music, Philadelphia, Pennsylvania. Interview with
    the Registrar. April, 1967.
Philadelphia Orchestra Association. Interviews and discussions took
    place with the following individuals: (a) all musicians who were
    members of the Orchestra from 1948 to 1967; (b) Board members
    Charles G. Berwind, Samuel Rosenbaum, Orville H. Bullitt, G.
    Ruhland Rebmann, Jr., Harry A. Batten, Henry P. McIlhenny, Mrs.
    Herbert C. Morris, E. A. Roberts, C. Wanton Balis, Jr., Mrs. James
    S. Hatfield, Jr., Stuart F. Loucheim, Bernard L. Frankel, Henry
    W. Sawyer, III, Hugh K. Duffield, Richard C. Bond; (c) managers
    Harl McDonald, Donald Engle, Roger Hall, Boris Sokoloff; (d)

Assistant Manager Joseph Santarlasci; (e) legal counsel Kenneth Souser, Park Dilks; (f) staff members Beth Parrish Glendinning, Wayne Shilkret, Florence Guion, Susan Kevis. October, 1948 to August, 1967.

————. Personal interview with Herman Kenin, President, American Federation of Musicians and Canada, New York, September, 1963.

————. Personal interview with Joseph Sharfsin, Esq., counsel for the Philadelphia Orchestra members. April, 1951.

————. Personal interview with Harry Shapiro, Esq., counsel for the Philadelphia Orchestra members. November, 1953.

————. Personal interview with Julian Goldberg, Esq., counsel for the Philadelphia Orchestra members. September, 1961.

————. Personal interview with Bernard Katz, Esq., counsel for the Philadelphia Orchestra members. September, 1966.

————. Personal interview with Michael Moskow, faculty member, School of Business Administration, Temple University. October, 1966.

————. Personal interview with Walter Gershenfeld, faculty member, School of Business Administration, Temple University. February, 1967.

————. Personal interview with Donald Yeager, Federal Mediation Service. February, 1967.

————. Personal interview with Harry Galfand, Esq., Labor Relations Advisor to the Mayor of Philadelphia. December, 1966.

————. Personal interview with Walter Powell, Management Consultant. February, 1967.

————. Personal interview with Leon Lunden, U. S. Department of Labor, Washington, D. C. March, 1967.

————. Personal interview with David Stone, Dean, Temple University College of Music, Philadelphia, Pennsylvania. October, 1968.

————. Personal interview with Sol Schoenbach, Director, Settlement Music Schools, Philadelphia, Pennsylvania. October, 1967.

————. Personal interview with Joseph Castaldo, composer and President of the Philadelphia Musical Academy, Philadelphia, Pennsylvania. September, 1968 and October, 1968.

————. Personal interview with Erich Leinsdorf, Conductor, Boston Symphony Orchestra, New York. December, 1966.

————. Personal interview with Daniel Webster, Music Critic, Philadelphia Inquirer. September, 1968.

————. Personal interview with George Rochberg, composer and

former chairman of the Music Department of the University of Pennsylvania, Philadelphia Pennsylvania. September, 1968.

————. Personal interview with George Zazofsky, member of the Boston Symphony Orchestra and President of the International Conference of Symphony and Opera Musicians (ICSOM), Philadelphia, Pennsylvania. November, 1965.

————. Personal interview with Digby Baltzell, Professor of Sociology, University of Pennsylvania, Philadelphia, Pennsylvania. September, 1968.

————. Personal interview with John Healy, Consultant on Fund Raising with G. A. Brakeley & Company, Inc. December, 1968.

————. Personal interview with Dr. Bernard Borislow, Consulting Psychologist. March, 1967.

————. Personal interview with Frederick R. Mann, President of Robin Hood Dell Concerts, Inc. and City Representative for the City of Philadelphia. October, 1963.

————. Personal interview with Morton Newman, Esq., member, Citizens' Committee to Save the Philadelphia Orchestra. December, 1962.

————. Personal interview with Paul Rosenbaum, consultant to Philadelphia Orchestra Pension Foundation. October, 1964.

————. Personal interview with Seymour Rosen, former Secretary of the American Symphony Orchestra League, Philadelphia, Pennsylvania. December, 1967.

————. Personal interview with Boris Sokoloff, manager of the Philadelphia Orchestra, Philadelphia, Pennsylvania. October, 1968.

————. Personal interview with Leonard Hale, Jerome Wigler, and Bert Phillips, members of the 1963 Philadelphia Orchestra members' committee, Philadelphia, Pennsylvania. January, 1965.

————. Personal interview with Joseph Santarlasci, assistant manager of the Philadelphia Orchestra, Philadelphia, Pennsylvania, December, 1967.

Index